NON-
NEGOTIABLE

TEN YEARS INCARCERATED—CREATING
THE UNBREAKABLE MINDSET

NON-NEGOTIABLE

TEN YEARS INCARCERATED—CREATING THE UNBREAKABLE MINDSET

Wes Watson

Published by Best Seller Publishing®, St. Augustine, FL
Best Seller Publishing® is a registered trademark.
Printed in the United States of America.
ISBN:978-1-956649-13-0

For more information, please write:
Best Seller Publishing®
53 Marine Street
St. Augustine, FL 32084
or call 1 (626) 765-9750
Visit us online at: www.BestSellerPublishing.org

TABLE OF CONTENTS

This book is dedicated to my beautiful wife, Valerie, and my baby boy, Wolfie, who give me the strength to fight everyday.

INTRODUCTION

My name is Wes Watson. Born and raised in San Diego, CA—Oceanside, to be exact. My town was built around Southern California culture, surfing, and skateboarding, but it also has a large drug and gang underworld influence. We grew up lower middle class, but my parents took great care of us and are still married to this day—which is one of the main influences that made me such a committed family man. I was a surfer/skater kid and I had a good-ass life. We had a nice house. My parents took really good fucking care of us. Great childhood. Great upbringing.

But then I started smoking weed. I didn't want to pay for that shit, so I started fucking hustling. I wanted that shit for free. All of a sudden, as a middleman, I started making a couple hundred per small sack. That evolved into pushing elbows (pound at a time). You gotta realize I was just a baby boy and those pounds being pushed per week escalated quickly into 100 packs and 200 packs a week. I validated myself in the most juvenile fashion, which was strictly external—no true core beliefs. I thought the car I drove and the money I had made me somebody, and man was I wrong.

People were driving fucking Honda Civics and shit that their parents paid for. Meanwhile, I got an Escalade on 23s. When the black Rover came out I didn't even wait ten minutes. I put the black fucking 23s on it, and I was killing on that one too.

But pushing those packs, I was making crazy fucking money. I was getting the British Columbia weed from Canada and, I mean, I'm making 400 bucks off each bow. I'm getting 200 at a time. Half's going to one homie. Half's going to the other. I'm making eighty grand a pop every fucking ten days. And so nobody could tell me shit. I thought I was the shit. Little did I know all of this was leading me down the wrong path.

Once the money's involved, shit goes bad—like, here comes the violence. I mean, I front someone. They front some other motherfucker. That fool's got problems paying. Then he gets a big mouth. All of a sudden the dude's splattered on the ground. He barely fucking makes it. Eight months later the U.S. marshals picked me up.

I stepped out of my friend's house, and I knew shit was off; there were some weird-ass people walking around and everything. Once I was outside, the marshals just had an AR-15 in my face—and boom, what's up? But I had been doing so much dirt at that time that I didn't know which reason brought them in front of me. Honestly, I thought it was for some other shit.

So, I really thought it was finished for me. I'm like, *Oh, life sentence, you're done.* Two days prior, something had happened that would have meant lights out for me. I would never wish these feelings upon anyone, knowing that your life's over at that moment. Some bearded dude in plain clothes is telling you he's a marshal service with the strap on you, and you know you did some fucked up shit two days ago. But then he tells me, "Man, you don't even know what this is for, do you?" And I go, "It's that violation, right?"

Well, the truth of the matter was that I had been ducking probation on a sales case. I got pulled over with 14 pounds in my trunk. At the time, that was like a 20-sack of weed to me; it was absolutely nothing compared to the weight we had been handling. When they pulled me over in my latest white Rover I told the cop, "Hey, don't scratch my fucking watch, man. That shit's worth more than fucking how much you made last year." He was pissed. I'm like, "I'm going to be out in twenty minutes anyways, so it don't even fucking matter."

But the point is, I signed for a joint suspension, which you don't want to do. So, I owed them five years right off the bat. I messed up my probation, and then the U.S. marshals came on this case. And so, when I brought it up, plain clothes said, "No, no, no. You're done." And he told me it was about a case where the guy fucking fronted some weight to this kid and some violence happened. Long story short, all parties testified against me.

Now, this kid is someone I showed the world to. He had a $4,000-a-month condo in Oceanside ($10,000 today). His fully furnished loft would blow your mind if you saw it. He had a Hummer—black-on-black. He had a Denali. He traveled to New York so he could do his thing over there, and then he'd come right back home on the regular. And this motherfucker snitched on me, tough as fuck. Everyone involved wanted to get me life so they would never see me again. People I showed the world to ….

I didn't see freedom for ten fucking years.

And really, that's just how it works, man. The second the authorities start throwing numbers like twenty-five years around, everyone cracks. It's that fucking song. It was all good just a week ago, when I was dropping money like it's nothing, paying for everyone's shit, driving the nicest car, living in the nicest house in Encinitas and the best condo in downtown San Diego. This week I was in cuffs, sitting in the front of a Dodge Ram, and the bearded U.S. marshal's got his computer there. I mean, fuck, I was just thinking, *Dude, I'm done. I'm done for life. I'm never getting out.* And from that day, I didn't see freedom for ten fucking years.

3

ONE SENTENCE
(MANY DIFFERENT STORIES)

I took my shit to trial. Why did I take my shit to trial? Because I had a joint suspension out of Orange County for a sales case. A joint suspension means you sign a deal that if you get in any trouble while on probation you need to go do the time. I previously needed to serve 180 days but got pulled out on a work furlough, and if I did anything during my probation I would serve four to five years.

They tried to offer me a low-ass deal in San Diego County— they wouldn't run the case concurrently with Orange County. Orange County is known for picking you up at the gate and making you do the joint suspension, so they were basically offering me what I got. Nevertheless, by going to trial and losing, I got about the same as I would have just signed for. If they would have run it concurrently I would've taken it, but they weren't saying they would. I had a good case, too. No fucks given on my part; they had no fucking real evidence on me. In the end, little did I know all this adversity I was going to overcome would become the foundation of me building my greatest internal assets.

"Ladies and gentlemen of the jury, how can we believe this new fucking fifteenth version of the story?"

In the end I could not win at trial. The victim told fourteen versions of his story to police. My lawyer went up there and made him run through every fucking version of the story. And at the end of the version, my lawyer had to say, "What about this story?" And the guy had to say, "Well, that was a lie." We ran through every single version in front of the jury and then my lawyer basically said, "Ladies and gentlemen of the jury, how can we believe this new fucking fifteenth version of the story?"

But they still convicted me with no hesitation; the system doesn't tell the jury how much time the defendant will be given. It just came down to whether or not I was guilty, and that verdict took two hours. They probably went down to PF Chang's and came back with full-ass stomachs, knowing they just washed me up. Meanwhile, I was sitting in the holding tank watching some burnt-ass movie (*Avatar*, actually) playing on repeat for hours as my life changed forever.

Today, the man who testified against me is in witness protection up north or something. He knew what the fuck he was doing. He knew the life he was living. The very first story he told police was that he got fucking jumped in Tijuana, Mexico, and he drove himself back to where he was found. That was the first version he told because he didn't want to admit he was doing dirt, too.

KEYS TO THE PATH
(CONSISTENCY, DEDICATION, AND LONG VIEW)

Many people don't get that when you go from county jail to reception in the pen, you'll sit there for three to four months without ever leaving the cell. They might give you yard time, but every time they open the yard it'll explode in violence because there's a lot of cleanup to do; a lot of people in that reception yard shouldn't be there, because their paperwork is bad. Every fucking time the door opens, someone's about to get "got" (meaning stabbed) and it doesn't matter if you're on A side, B side, or C side of the building, you're just praying, *Oh, shit. Hopefully, I make it out to yard today.* And then, all of a sudden, you hear the fucking sirens wailing that someone is getting stabbed or beat up and you ain't making it out to yard at all. So, you start off your term with a three- to four-month stay in a cell with your celly starving, very rarely leaving.

---

*I would be the best at prison life by
getting swole AF and blasted AF.*

In all honesty, I prepared myself mentally by not fucking with drugs—nothing. I stayed physically active, working out every fucking day. I read books on self-improvement. I just always wanted to better myself because I knew that (a) this wasn't my future, and (b) I'm the type of person who knows he'll be best at whatever he does. So, while in there I would be the best at prison life by getting swole AF and blasted AF. I'm not gonna lie. I always say "Acquire what you admire," and I always admired being big, ripped, and blasted. On top of that, I would shape the guys around me to be the best they could be as well. Ultimately, that was accomplished by staying clean, grinding hard with the workouts, staying mentally positive, and just focusing on the thought that there would be a future for each of us. Right now, we're going to do what we got to do.

Testament to that, there was a hot-ass day I remember clear as *fuck* on the yard at Donovan, the level four yard. My homeboy Jammer from DAGO (prison gang name for San Diego Car) was an old school cat—big old whip (handlebar mustache) and a cold convict stroll. He had been down forever; he's not getting out. While I'm on the yard, a correctional officer (CO) pulls me over and he goes, "Hey, Watson. Check this out." And I go, "Hey, what's up, sir?"

"Wait one second." He points to the line where inmates report for kitchen work. "Your homeboy (COs really talk like they're gangster, trust me) has walked around that corner at this time every day for fourteen years. Watch this. He's going to be the first guy around that corner." And I wait and I'm like,

Bullshit. But then, *Oh fuck, here he comes* .... Practically on the dot, he stepped around that corner. I was struck by Jammer's level of consistency and dedication.

I would aim to be the most consistent
man alive as long as I lived.

The fact that a cop was noticing this in an inmate was just huge to me and it sparked something in me that I will never forget. Jammer would work the scullery, washing dishes for eight to fourteen hours. And he'd do that shit with a smile on his face—the extra meal at the end of the day sure as fuck helped. He looked forward to it because he saw the work itself as a gift; it brought peace and contentment to his heart. From that moment forward, I knew I would aim to be the most consistent man alive as long as I lived.

Very few, if anyone, out here on the streets has a long view like that. And really, that kind of long view is the key to success in everything. Can you see ten years? Can you see fourteen years? Hell, if I ask someone if they can see four years, they can't. But Jammer came around that corner every day at that time for fourteen years without fail to go work a minimal job most would consider unbearable, just to keep his mind right. That's deep as fuck to me. As I love to say, "The man who takes more pride in the steps to attain the result than the result itself cannot be stopped. The work truly instills the worth."

In any given process, getting through the steps brings contentment; the result does not. Just as Jammer received some peace of fucking mind cleaning plates and shit, I applied the mindset to everything I was doing. As I worked on myself, I avoided focusing on the result and instead focused on the steps, the process. We should consistently live in a manner we admire, and that's what I was doing through exercise, reading, and self-improvement.

"The man who takes more pride in the steps to attain the result than the result itself cannot be stopped. The work truly instills the worth."

By living it, I began personifying my beliefs. And my beliefs are consistency, dedication, and not about trying to just acquire. People are trying to acquire instead of *become*. If you're here for that same reason, you need to ask yourself a very important question. Do you want to become strong, or do you just want to appear to be (mentally and physically)?

I really just want to be what I appear to be and not be, through and through! Successful people have sets of principles that make them successful. It's not just that they have money. A lot of people have money. It doesn't mean they're successful. Yeah, I might see the money at first, but then I want to see the principles. I want to know where they really came from, where the origin was, and the origin being these same principles that go across the board: consistency, dedication, fortitude, and everything that makes a man a man.

MY TRUE INTENTIONS

Over a decade later, I found a dude laughing at me at the gym for filming my workout because he thinks he's a badass. I pulled him over and said, "Hey listen, man. I like that mirror. I like these weights. And I like how this makes me feel. I like filming my workout. Guess what? I didn't have a fucking mirror for ten years. Do you know what that feels like?"

And the dude was looking at me like, *Damn*, and I pulled up on him like, "I'm not shook by you at all. So, I don't think you understand. I'm going to teach you something one way or another, and I care that you walk out of here without that weird-ass attitude, because this is a positive place."

This is more than a workout for me. It's sure as fuck more than appearance. My training is mainly based on Instagram (@Watson_Fit). My work changes lives. Really. Plenty of fucking people I know. I've had them quit drinking and doing drugs to start pursuing a healthier lifestyle, listening to their fucking hearts, and following their visions. I'm like, "Motherfucker, when you wake up in the morning, are you stoked with where you're at? If you're not, you need to make the changes."

A big lesson for me is that "Regret is your guideline." If you did something and you regret it, that's your inner voice telling you how to live your best life. That's your conscience guiding you! The universe is encouraging you, trying to keep your actions in *alignment* with your life's purpose so you can fulfill your destiny while on this earth.

---

*I wish there were stuff like that when I was being
a fucking idiot. It would have saved me from
a lot of unneeded pain I caused myself.*

For the readers who don't know me just yet, I started posting videos when I was still in penitentiary. A lot of those old posts are still up, and I always put up something positive. I stay the humble route. I'm never pushing anything other than let's be the best version of ourselves that we can be. A lot of my posts will help correct you on the daily. Honestly, just because you know the right thing in this exact moment, that doesn't mean you'll know it when you're in the wrong fucking state of mind. I wish there were stuff like that when I was being a fucking idiot. It would have saved me from a lot of unneeded pain I caused myself.

After my ten-year stay, and after furthering my passion, I'm now sharing that positivity and humility through my book. I appeal to different types of people, but mainly to people into the personal growth space. Again, I share my discipline on my Instagram, @Watson_Fit. Every day, I show that I'm up at 2:45 AM and at the gym by 4:00 AM. I show my dedication at a different level because discipline is truly the prerequisite to success.

Stay focused, choose the correct daily habits, and you will go straight to the top.

A lot of people talk shit on social media. I'm like, "Well, you better watch what you're putting out there because you're drawing in what you're putting out." I truly want people to do better and my approach is the *hard truths* that snap us out of our comfort zones. And the people around me can feel that. That's the effect of the vibe you put out there with your true intentions at heart. My true intentions are to show you all the following: don't fucking get caught up in the bullshit life based on perpetual pleasure-chasing that leads to ten years, if not a lifetime, of just torture, like I did. Stay focused, choose the correct daily habits, and you will go straight to the top.

So, I ask you, and be honest:

Are you content with where you are mentally, physically, spiritually, and financially?

Are you fucking *content*?

If not, then it's time for some changes. Your best life is non-negotiable. Your *vision* is NOT up for fucking debate. Over the course of these pages, I want to help you understand how you can make the necessary changes for improvement.

Always follow your vision.

Don't take no for an answer.

Let's enjoy the freedom of discipline.

1

THE GUIDANCE OF REGRET

(Why the Fuck You Keep Quitting)

Being on the streets, things are very different than in the penitentiary. It seems like *every* fucking time I go into the gym lately, some motherfucker has a problem with something I'm doing. I know what it is. They've probably fucking done some background research and they've already made their mind up on me. But one thing for sure is I'm never going to make the mistake of trying to explain myself to people who are committed to misunderstanding me.

Please, always understand this. Some people are committed to misunderstanding you, and all you need to do is wish them growth, wish them understanding, give them their needed space, and send love their way. We're not going to understand it. Maybe they're just having a bad day, and we're not going to let that affect us. We're going to go right through our Monday, stick to the plan, and create that Positive Mental Attitude (PMA) with our actions. Always create your momentum and drive with your actions; don't worry about something someone else is doing.

It should be no secret: I'm a massive, massive mother-fucking believer in energy exchanges. Our actions and our energy dictate how people feel about us subconsciously. I want everyone to have a good positive feeling about me, and I want to feel that way about them. I've lived around all the negativity in the fucking world. Even as a very successful person I still had negativity.

---

*Our actions and our energy dictate how
people feel about us subconsciously.*

If we fucking cultivate positivity, this is the only chance we're ever going to have at a life that is consistently blessing us. Ultimately, I cannot tell how positive you are when everything's going your way. The truth is that I wait for a negative situation to arise, and then I see how people act. What momentum and motivation are you fucking capable of cultivating when life isn't exactly ideal? This is what matters most.

Our problems make us. A lot of this soft-ass shit is tripping me the fuck out. Grown-ass, soft-ass men. Princess-ass motherfuckers wanting it easier, wanting a day off, and crying over their problems. Motherfucker, your problem is that you think one day you're not going to have fucking problems! So, check it out. I know my motherfucking place on this earth. I'm the fucking reminder. To these people, I'm the fucking reminder because I don't forget that my problems fucking made me.

Every time I'm coming to some issue, I just see it as this is life happening *for* me. This is my level-up. I don't want it easier. This is the self-talk that builds champions, the self-talk I need you to have.

---

*I lived without your problems for so long
that my perspective shifted entirely.*

Just the other day, I saw two dudes slacking like a mother-fucker in life while talking about a football game they saw on TV. I couldn't help but wonder how the fuck we glorify all competition except when it's the competition with our mother-fucking selves to level up and step the fuck over our problems. Why the fuck don't people see that bitch-ass shit? They never had no real problems? Or they're just never truly present for them. As you enter different stages of growth, as you start to develop a higher level of awareness, you begin to realize we as humans cannot resolve issues in the same mindset in which the problem was created. It truly takes someone like myself who comes from a place where the problems of society don't exist. I lived without your problems for so long that my perspective shifted entirely.

As humans, we naturally look for issues. This is how we stay leveling up. This is our progression. Internal progression comes from overcoming issues. So, even if you have nothing you will look for issues. And when there are no surface issues, because you're in isolation or solitary, you'll fucking seek the internal ones. So, coming from a different place, a different mindset, seeking internal solutions, I have the fucking answer.

None of these problems you think you have are external in nature.

You don't have a money issue; you have an issue with discipline and an issue with being able to sacrifice. You don't have a fucking fitness issue; you have an issue with discipline and an issue with being able to sacrifice. Do you fucking get it? You don't have the external problems you think you have; you have problems with your internal values and principles. We must attack the problem at the root, not looking at the supposed tangible issue but by strengthening our core principles. Fact is, you could be as rich as you want and as ripped as you want right now off of everything you currently have IF you are disciplined enough, IF you can sacrifice enough, IF you can suffer enough, long enough. So the long view is the key.

I hear it right now as I put these words on the fucking page. I hear the whiners. I hear the bitches who are ready to tap out. I hear the fake motherfuckers. "But Wes, Wes, it's not about just being ripped and being rich ...." Sure, but it is about progression, motherfucker. It's about respecting yourself, and if you don't progress in life you will not respect yourself.

So, guess what? The correct *internal* principles will cause you to get more ripped. The correct *internal* principles will get you the financial security you always dreamt of. You will learn to sacrifice more. You'll be more dedicated. You'll be more consistent. You'll look to the future more in a positive manner devoid of the anxiety caused by inaction. These are the principles I create.

Someone who just lives in the moment, like "It's just about being happy"—they will always fuck themselves. They're not planning enough. If that's you, then you're not planning enough ahead. You're not preparing enough each day by strengthening your principles. You're not realizing that your progression dictates how you love and respect your life.

COGNITION & SELF-INVESTMENT

Everyone is working backward.

People will say, "Never give up, keep pushing," all this shit, and they're only applying it to the physical realm. The main place I care about you applying this is to cognition. Everyone is working backward. They're starting with intensity, then they're going to consistency. And then when that doesn't work they finally try to gather knowledge. I want it done the other way. Gather knowledge, then apply consistency, then kick up your intensity.

Sometimes people will be shocked with the way I speak, or my ability to string together complex thoughts, or the cognitive capacity I keep. But the thing is, it's all simple because the same wisdom applies to all areas of life; the way we do anything is the way we do everything. So, when a thought enters my mind, I never give up on trying to comprehend it. I have a deep need to process it, to understand it at the highest level, and ultimately to apply it to my situation internally and externally.

The area that is massively obvious to me is at the gym. I'll see someone I know who operates at a high level in a different area of life, but then they come into the gym and it all goes out the fucking window. They start throwing weights around and they're just in the physical realm. There is no forethought. There is no planning. Their cognitive function is nonexistent. And this is why we fucking need to have solid principles and apply them across the board. We don't just drop principles in one area because we're telling ourselves, "Oh, that's not my area." No. Your area is principles, your wisdom and understanding, and applying them across the board.

Something that always strikes me is an intellectual who has trouble maintaining, acquiring, or building a certain physique. If you're an intellectual, you should understand this very easily; it's an extremely basic topic. It seems extremely contradictory how we can let our health fail as supposed intellectuals. I mean, what do we all want? More confidence. How can anyone not pursue what we all want? And how do we get it? Through the fucking work. The work truly instills the worth.

The only thing that gives you confidence is the work you put in. Your self-worth is directly correlated to your self-investment. I don't care how good of shape people think I'm in. If I don't go to the gym, if I don't structure my meals correctly, if I don't work to earn the confidence in correlation to my known capacity for building my desired aesthetics, then I won't be fucking confident. Simple as that!

The work truly instills the worth.

Everything is earned internally and externally. It doesn't matter how I look. It's how I *feel*. Everything is about how we feel, and we only feel 100 percent confident when we earn it through self-investment. A high level of self-worth is through self-investment, and always working toward being the best version of ourselves in every way.

SOLITARY MIND
(REGRET IS NOT A CHOICE)

Isolation. Isolation will teach you everything about yourself. They say the conscience is the speaking of the soul with itself. When you sit down for 3,000-plus days, your internal dialogue is going to surpass anything you ever knew. The biggest thing that got me through massive, massive stretches of isolation was the fact that I began to pinpoint my imaginary evils and finally realize they were incurable.

I had this logged in the back of my head: *Wes, imaginary evils are incurable.* I learned to just choose the outcome and the situation that suited my mindset the best when I was in that negative situation—you know when you're just skipping too far ahead and you're just making shit up, believing it, and running a train in your own mind with it. Everyone does it out here. They sit there in a negative mindset, they make some shit up, they believe a fictional scenario based on miniscule amounts of truth, and they fuck their days off. Why do we all do this? And how do we combat it?

Defeating a negative mindset while in such a negative place is far from fucking easy.

It will only come from someone who lived the most negative days possilbe in the world and overcame them in a positive way, to not only survive in such a negative place but thrive. Motherfucker, I'm talking about the SHU (segregated housing unit). I'm talking about long stretches on lockdown. I'm not talking about knives and fights and all that shit. That shit becomes second nature in the pen. But dealing with yourself? Defeating a negative mindset while in such a negative place is far from fucking easy. But it's definitely possible and here is how I did it.

I got up every morning at 2:45 AM. I went straight into some positive reading, then directly into a workout. I conducted myself like the man I admired. If I didn't put my whole heart into that workout, if I failed to fully achieve a flow state during my morning routine, I knew I had to focus more and let go. I was preparing every day because life was coming and I would be ready mentally and physically. I knew plenty of guys behind those locked doors didn't get up at program time. They broke it down and laid it back down. They didn't really work out, and that was evident in their physiques when the doors opened. I told myself every day I would not be this motherfucker. If anything, I was out to earn my own love and respect.

---

*You need to stay present for the pain, and
that's when the level-up occurs.*

A motherfucker who does ten years should look like a motherfucker who did ten years. If your boy comes out, he says he did fifteen and he's got the titties, he's got the tats, and he's got the fucking spare tire, you know how he did his time. He rode that rack, needle hanging out the arm. He was sucking on some fucking Little Debbie's and that's just what it is. Fucking people can do a gang of time, but they're not really doing time. Their time is doing them, because they're not present. You need to stay present for the pain, and that's when the level-up occurs. You wait till that moment. You can't take one more second of that pain, that torture. That's when you flip the timer on.

All too often, I was stuck in my dark-ass, wet, shitty-ass cell where it was snowing outside and dripping water from the ceiling. Stuck in there, thinking, *What type of fucked up shoddy-ass construction is this?* There's water dripping and the walls are sweating to where you put up some pictures and they go sliding down the fucking wall. *Motherfucker!* Nine times out of ten you're sticking the shit to the wall with toothpaste, or maybe you can get some bond wood glue from the shop. But anyways the fucking point is, dig deep within the second you can't fucking take no more. Anticipate these times you can't take no more! When you're really about to crack and have those gems like "Life happens for us" instilled in your mind— your self-talk at that moment is who the fuck you are. Not breaking is your level-up.

You ain't that person when you're all pumped up, with all that liquid courage running through your system, and fucking thinking you're badass. When it gets impossibly hard, you're that motherfucker who decides to stand the fuck up at that moment or bitch the fuck out. I did time with them all. Face-tatted murderers, high-level street gang leaders who didn't come out looking like me and I don't give a fuck if they did or not. I don't care how they look. I want to know that their character shaped their external figure, their aesthetics.

You look a certain way if you live a certain way. I know motherfuckers who made such drastic gains internally and externally so quick. In the pen, you can undo karmic debt (more on this in Chapter 2) at a level you could never do out here because you're not getting into the bullshit. So many people are blocking themselves in daily life with these tiny little vices, these tiny amounts of karmic debt just being thrown in their way. You might be looking at them like, "Oh, fucking Johnny's a good dude. Why can't he just get ahead? That motherfucker's got buzzard luck or some shit. Everything bad always happens to him." Well, it's because he's throwing little bits of karmic debt in his way and he's never able to get ahead because the universe has it out on him. Like, "Hey motherfucker, act right, act right!"

It could be something as small as "Johnny's true intentions that are holding him back." You don't know nobody's real true intentions. If you see one of those motherfuckers who is constantly failing, never really getting anywhere, you might want to look a little deeper into their daily fucking activities. The point is, you can build up karmic debt just by not even being your best self, by not walking in line with your conscience—or following the vision supplied by the universe—due to your selfish desires.

"Fuck, Wes, you're making it look like a motherfucker would envy you to be in prison. What the fuck?"

Your path is your conscience. I hate when people say, "Oh, I don't regret nothing. Even the mistakes I made, I don't regret them." Fuck, I've said that. I've said I don't regret the time I did this and that, but this is the fucking difference: I didn't regret it then. I did my time, and just as I live today, I did it in a voyeuristic manner. I sit in the back of my head and I watch myself. I had many people write me during that time and say, "Fuck, Wes, you're making it look like a motherfucker would envy you to be in prison. What the fuck?" It's because I was living my story. I was and always remained fucking present. I'm not looking anywhere else other than where I'm at. Where I'm at is the place I should be, and I'm extracting growth from the present moment.

Regret is not a choice.

What I'm trying to tell you is that regret is not a choice. When people say "I don't regret this" or "I do regret that," it's not a fucking choice, because a lot of people lie. Your regret is your guideline to be your best motherfucking self. Regret is simply placed in your head by your conscience telling you how to motherfucking act. When you regret something, there's something that needs to be removed. Simple as that! It's a fucking hookup from the universe, from your conscience. They refer to the conscience as the authentic voice of God, of the universe. Adherence to your conscience is your path.

Until you learn to walk in line with your conscience, to live in congruence with it, you will forever be plagued by your thoughts, your actions, and your choices. You will not fucking feel whole. You will feel off because you are off. You're making choices based on stuff other people fucking think and any sort of external influences that aren't coming from your heart. Then the regrets hit you, after the actions and the fucking choices you make. In all reality the biggest problem we as humans cause ourselves is trying to convince our minds of something our heart knows is a lie.

Anything that causes regret needs to be expelled at once, but isolation is a different motherfucker because of those incurable evils, those things we make up, not the simple changeable actions we regret in our everyday lives. How do we combat these destructive scenarios we are making up in our own heads that drain our energy and cripple us physically?

"Why?" is one of the evilest things
when done in a negative way.

It will always be the selfless route that combats incurable evils. The incurable evils, to me, were negative thought patterns when I was wondering, *Why don't my parents come visit me? Why don't people write me? Do these motherfuckers care about me?* That question "Why?" is one of the evilest things when done in a negative way. When we ask "Why?" with our internal dialogue in a negative way, it can fucking kill us; it can take our fucking life.

I sat there for so long asking why, and I finally just said, "Fuck it. Fuck why. I love them anyway. I don't care why. I'm going to rewrite this narrative in my head and take the selfless route. I don't need anything to give them my love. I'm going to learn unconditional love the hard way in the hardest place. Then I'm going to pass it on to everyone I love. I'm going to need less and love more."

The second I did that, everything went away. I wasn't blaming; instead, I automatically took the fucking champion chair and fucking left the victim one for them other bitches who need to stick needles in their arms to get through the fucking day. And trust, I feel their pain. I've been a dope fiend;

it's painful. I've chased every fucking way of just leaving and altering my consciousness. Nothing fucking worked but the *hard truths*! That's what got me in check, so I teach the way I learned.

I wasn't blaming; instead, I automatically took the fucking champion chair and fucking left the victim one for them other bitches who need to stick needles in their arms to get through the fucking day.

Just getting fucking high, you ain't even present for pain. How can you understand it and grow beyond it? That shit is so pussy to me. When I see a motherfucker who needs to get drunk—as in they must, or else they have no true confidence—I don't even see drinking as someone enjoying themselves. I'm like, "Damn, what are you running from?" When I see someone using any vices to escape their reality, I'm like, "Fuck, it's that bad?"

Anything that you're getting from this external substance that's creating a certain pattern of thought in your head—or erasing it—you can do on your own without the substance by, first, just believing you can and then, second, by creating habits to construct strengths on the other side of your weaknesses. By continually trying to conduct yourself in a social manner without the alcohol, to relax without the weed, you can do it on your own.

But guess what! Guess what! Guess the fuck what! Like everything else on this planet, you've got to fucking earn it. Habitual construction is *real*. How do you earn it? Long view. You ain't getting it in year one. You ain't getting it in year two. You ain't getting it in year five. You ain't. Are you ready for year eight? Are you ready for year ten? Are you going to realize that you don't even have it at year fifteen?

You're still at 75 percent of getting it, and you're ready to keep going. Those motherfuckers who will never give up on what they truly want will make it through isolation. They'll seek isolation when they get out. They know their elevation requires isolation and a man is more useful when he travels alone because he reflects more. They'll seek solitude when they get out because they know they'll find all their answers in solitude.

In the SHU, you get 55 bucks worth of canteen. That ain't even enough to get a few fucking soaps, a jar of coffee, and a few fucking top ramens. This is what you're getting for your 55 bucks a month: you starve. They're putting you in the optimal state and all I have to say about that is, "THANK YOU!"

The internal attributes I created made me impervious to defeat.

Thank you, state of California! Thank you! You put me in the optimal state for so many years to turn me into the man I needed to be—to become my best self. You put me in solitude. You starved me. You made me face those impossibly hard times. You threw adversity in my way. And guess what? I didn't fuckin' crack. And you know what else? The internal attributes I created made me impervious to defeat.

So, now we're winning.

MOTIVATION

People think motivation is like pixie dust or some shit. You don't just stumble upon motivation; everything is created from within. Motivation is created when we combine action with positive self-talk. I have created someone who is unstoppable by having a high level of awareness toward my internal dialogue, consistently magnifying it while in pursuit of my goals. Through our actions and our self-talk, we are the ones creating our strengths and weaknesses.

I was stuck in a cell by myself for twenty-three hours a day, and nobody was walking by except the cop who's counting or handing me my fucked-up-ass tray of slop that I don't even want to eat. But that presented another challenge, didn't it? Taking down that food and eating only the macronutrients on that tray that I knew would benefit me. So, I was sitting there just eating the meat and my self-talk just drifts to *Nobody can fucking eat like me. No one can suffer like me. No one will take pride in the sacrifice like me.* I was creating that machine from within, just taking pride and pleasure in my ability to not be pleased—all while existing in the most negative place on Earth.

When we make it harder on ourselves,
we respect our goals more.

The man who can take pride and get pleasure from not being pleased is unstoppable. The common denominator of successful people is their ability to do as many things a day as fucking possible to get where they want to go, regardless of how they fucking feel about the task at hand. So, check those feelings at the fucking gate. Check them at the gym. Check them at the park. Check them at the bars. Check them at that wake-up time. I don't give a fuck. Make it hard on yourself. When we make it harder on ourselves—when we take the harder route, when we put more into our goals, more love, more consistency, more effort—we respect our goals more.

When we respect our goals more, it means more to us to stick to them. It's nothing you'll read or hear. It's experience. It's soul-searching. It's digging deeper during times of adversity. It's how you speak to yourself and how you act through your thoughts and through your actions. It's you. You are creating your personal strengths and your weaknesses. When people say, "But Wes, I'm just lacking motivation …." I say, "Why the fuck are you talking to yourself like that? Why are you putting yourself in a deficit? Why are you making yourself a victim?"

I never tell myself that. I just fucking go. Just go. Just go and make it a habit. When we habitually construct habits, we completely rewire our subconscious. When we rewire our subconscious, we get rid of what's plaguing everyone out here. What's plaguing everyone out here? Cognitive dissonance. This is when your subconscious mind knows you're a fucking liar.

When you have conflicting belief systems in your mind, you know you want something, but your subconscious knows you don't do it and it knows your self-talk isn't aligned with the actions you're taking to create the future you desire, the strengths you wish to possess. So embrace the fact that repetition is strength, *repetition* is key, and get over those fucking feelings about what you want to do, never hesitating on what you need to do.

I regularly post videos of my routine. I'm posting this shit over and over and over and over. The same workout, same food, all this shit over and over and over. This is how we fucking develop a greater degree of comprehension. How are you going to comprehend something if you switch it up due to your likes or dislikes? I don't give a fuck if you like it or not. In all fucking honesty—in total fucking transparency—learning to like the shit that's best for you, that you don't like to fucking do, this is how we fucking defeat every problem out here.

People think they'll just take a pill—or someone will magically just do some fucking ceremony on them or something—and they're going to fucking snap out of it. Fuck no! You snap yourself out of it. The universe blesses you for your hard work and your commitment. You get the power and develop clarity because you put the work in, because you put the blood, sweat, and tears in.

You don't need to be fucking Arnold Schwarzenegger. You don't need to be the richest man in the world. But your daily motherfucking plan should be progressing you in every way. If there's no progression, there is no pride. If there is no fucking progression, there's only regression. And, as far as I'm concerned, there is no stagnation. When you regress— when you choose to regress—you know what you're doing to yourself. It's no secret. The second I choose not live my fucking plan or follow through with my fucking vision, my self-talk goes negative too. What's the difference? I automatically call myself a bitch, negating any doubt and fear that develops within by taking immediate action.

I owe everybody out here the strength that I can give by living it, by personifying the teaching. And no, I don't fucking mean telling people how to live. I fucking show them. I am the example. I share the steps. I love you guys when you start loving yourselves and putting that investment in yourselves, when you start to create motivation from within—fucking positivity, self-worth, self-love. When you start to create that from within, you'll pass it on to your family, and when you pass it on to your family, they'll pass it on too. This is how we raise global vibration and create a strong collective consciousness in our network.

We can unmake the fucking problems of this world by simply being a collective consciousness. We are one. We are all one. And we are fucking this shit up. We are!

I was the biggest problem. I thought the result was everything. Like, *What do I do? Oh—get this car or get this pad and it's going to mean so much to me!* Motherfucker, it's not the possessions we attain along the path. It's the man who's created. So don't fucking short-change the path. Make it fucking harder. Just because you went to the penitentiary and you had this realization doesn't mean shit if you didn't make it progressively harder and stay present during the pain.

When you have no choice, it's immensely more fucking complicated. And when you suddenly have no choice, it's so easy to be a victim.

If you make your trials in life easy, when you come back and bring what you learned back to the real world, you're too soft. The real world is hard. The real world is fucking hard. Prison is fucking harder. It's the hardest version of the real world. People always liken me to these other motivators and I'm like, they had a choice, motherfucker. They had a choice. When you have a choice, it's different. When you have no choice, it's immensely more fucking complicated. And when you suddenly have no choice, it's so easy to be a victim.

Most people in prison are victims. *Oh, I can't do that because I'm here.* And it's an obvious/okay excuse. That's the thing about excuses. It's an obvious excuse, but that's the thing about excuses. But the fact is, you don't need to fall victim to them. You can either be a victim and have excuses or you can be that fucking champion motherfucker who has solutions.

There are problems in life. When you find solutions to them, you fucking win. I had to go through fucking fifty steps to track my macros and get ripped in prison. To get started, I needed to get a phone. I needed to research that shit. I needed to put the phone away and charge the battery, which is a massive task to undergo while holding contraband in the penitentiary.

Five motherfuckers had to go to the fucking chow hall to bag their food up so that I could get my 50 grams of protein per meal. And I needed to trade them something else for it. I needed to order them something else from a package weeks ahead of time or have it all planned out with each individual which items they would receive and make sure they got them. Fuck it, ninety steps. Just to hit my macros daily and stay ripped to ultimately come out and make this coaching vision a reality.

And those ninety steps are what keep me to my goals to this very fucking day. The amount I sacrificed and the amount of work I put in to get where I'm at is what keeps me fucking here. If you want the easy road, you're fucked. The *easy path* means it'll be easier to deter. Anytime I see someone seeking the easy road, I know it won't fucking last for them. And I want for them to have what I created for myself.

It's the most fucking power in the world: self-control and self-discipline. I want them to do it the hardest way because that's the way they'll fucking learn. I'll give you exactly as much as you need to connect the dots because then you'll learn it and you won't need me. And then you can pass it on.

When you teach, eventually your pupil will hopefully fucking surpass you. I've had them surpass me. And what happened? They've taught me. They re-fucking-gave me the power on days when I needed it. All of us are fallible. Life is. But the fact is there are so many fucking things that are fully under your control to be perfect at. So that excuse of nobody's perfect only falls in the situations that aren't completely under your control. But choosing this fucking snack over that healthy food, or fucking sleeping in over waking early to create your best self every fucking day? That's completely under your control and I'm continually shocked how people think self-mastery starts with complex topics and not the basics.

I know the key to everything in this life is mastering each day, then stringing together perfect days.

Fuck your feelings about the task. Fuck everything about it. Fuck it. The only thing you should worry about is the people. Your people. I'll continue saying this because you are my people. I won't sleep in because of you guys. I know if I sleep in, then five people will chose to sleep in, too, and fuck that. Fuck that. I know the key to everything in this life is mastering each day, then stringing together perfect days.

This changed my world. I went from being the worst motherfucker you can imagine to a man who won't physically harm a soul. Now you come at my family, it's a different fucking story. I'm going to do life if someone harms them, but why state the obvious? Anyway, I'm a different person now. When I even yell at someone now, when I even come out of character and raise my voice, it hurts me. It bothers me. It takes time away from my life. Karmic debt ensues, and I am punished internally.

This is emotional maturity, spiritual growth, and adherence to universal truth, knowing that we must give what we want in return so that we can live our best life, so that we can be productive. All you productive motherfuckers out there who take so much pride in your productivity, pass it on. Pay it forward. And realize that you don't have time for negativity; it just takes away from your energy going into your positive acts. I fucking love when I see a motherfucker win and the only way to win in life and achieve the success and inner peace we're all after is through positive thoughts and actions.

2

PICK YOUR SIDE

(Fake-Hard, or Paying Karmic Debt)

Let's just get straight into it. We don't have to live this lie no more. If you ain't proud of your conduct, if you ain't proud of where you're at, they ain't either. Your family ain't proud. Your girl ain't proud. Your kids aren't proud. You don't have to continue conducting yourself like that. This is a motherfucking choice.

Your lack of investment in yourself is so much more disrespectful than any fucking words I could ever speak or will express in this book.

All too often the biggest mistake I see is motherfuckers trying to give away a product (themselves) to their people, without even being proud of it themselves. Trying to toss themselves off onto people like, "Hey, hey, look at this shit I put absolutely NO work into … You want it?" So many motherfuckers out here all trying to be all politically correct *not* to hurt a princess-motherfucker's feelings. Straight-up. Your lack of investment in yourself is so much more disrespectful than any fucking words I could ever speak or will express in this book. So the fact is, get used to the hard truths of life so you can reflect upon them and level up.

Get this shit straight. I invest in myself because I respect my people. I want them to be proud of me. I'm not fucking passing them off some guilt-based shit like, "Oh, you have to take me. I'm your family ... You have to accept me." Such a shame how many individuals out here force their people to compromise their integrity and lie to them because of pure laziness. The only thing keeping you from being your best self and the best person for your people is your selfish desires.

Stick the needle in your arm—or get the fuck up and go work? Eat this fucking pastry—or eat the fucking chicken and some rice? Come on, man. If there's a motherfucking thing you want in this life and you ain't getting it, it's because you're fucking choosing pleasure over purpose and not connecting the dots like a bitch. And that's why my program works so fucking well, because every time you're about to make those choices not in line with the future you desire, you can just go ahead and call yourself a bitch because you know it fits.

I've been that shot-out motherfucker at the bottom, forgot about, a straight-up California Department of Corrections number, nothing more, wondering if I could ever bring my shot-out ass up from the fucking pit I threw myself in. So, it was one simple fact, one simple thing that I kept in my head:

I'm not a bitch. Watch this shit. Watch me do it. You know what? Fuck what I want. I know what I need to do. Make my people proud.

Make your fucking people proud today.

Get that shit.

WE PAY FOR WHAT WE DO

From the beginning of my case, the district attorney had it out for me. She kept telling me to take the deal or they were gonna hang me. I had a case that was chock-full of reasonable doubt. The victim fucking told at least fifteen different versions of the same story to the police. By the time he gave his fourteenth version of the story, my lawyer had already said, "No, we're going to blow this dude's story out of the water. He's changed his story so many times there's no way they're going to take this beyond a reasonable doubt."

So, I basically told the DA, "I'm not taking any deal. Your guys don't have a case. The victim, the person who's going to be pointing the finger at me, he's told so many different versions of the story that there's no way the jury is going to believe this fifteenth version."

My lawyer made him walk through every version of the story. When he would question the victim about a new version, he would ask, "So what about this version?" And the guy legitimately said, "Oh, well. That was a lie." And then the fifteenth version arrived, finally. My lawyer said, "Okay, well, this story that you're telling now to the jury, this is the real story that you want us to go forward and prosecute this man, Mr. Watson, on?" And the victim said, "Yeah, this one I'm telling the truth." And the jury still believed him. They still convicted me.

The point is, the DA had it out for me the whole time. She knew the other codefendants and the victim were getting less than a year in prison. She knew they were going to give me the full exposure, which was twenty-eight years and ended up being nine years after sentencing. Later, I ended up catching another year in-house (which means "in prison") doing a total of ten years incarcerated. I didn't know it at the time, but the DA's karmic debt was starting to build into her own sentence.

She knew I should not have gotten ten years. Everybody else in the case got a year. Why did she give me ten years?

It turned out she had done stuff like that to chalk up man years and increase convictions. This had been going on for fucking years, but then one day it really just caught up with her and she couldn't take it no longer. On November 11, 2011, she sent out some emails to the county, basically saying that she could not deal with the guilt any longer. She was found in her vehicle during a traffic stop and she had a gun in her hand. As the officer was telling her to put the gun down she blew her own head off.

Karmic debt will fucking strike you back
when you do people wrong.

I feel there's an inescapable truth to her story. Karmic debt will fucking strike you back when you do people wrong. If you're not following universal laws like karmic debt and the golden rule, you will receive whatever it is you put out there. If you take people's lives, your life will be taken. If you take a large portion of someone's life, well, guess what? You'll lose a large portion of yours. And I'm sure from what happened to the DA that she probably took a lot of people's actual lives to where it ended up being an eye for an eye. What she gave them, what she took, she got back in the end. And the fact was she just couldn't deal with herself, with how horrible of a person she had become through the prosecutorial system.

In a dark turn of events, the same thing happened to the codefendant in my case. He ended up getting shot two years later. The codefendant, a kid I raised my whole life, who I taught how to make money, taught how to live his life on his own terms, ended up getting shot in the stomach on my birthday. He told police he shot himself when he was pulling a gun from his holster, but it was repercussions from the street life he was living, not what he told police. He's the one who pointed the finger at me in court and told the jury that I was the one who did it. He sat and testified against me. He claimed he was in fear of me and that I would kill him if they let me out so they shouldn't even let me out. And this is a friend of mine. Man, people really show their true colors when facing a lot of time.

So, on 11/11/11 the DA's karmic debt caught up to her. And a year later, on my birthday, it caught up to the codefendant, too. These remain significant dates to me, when karmic debt was dished out according to how those people treated me.

We need to pay for what we do in
this life. Karma is a mirror.

Ultimately, I don't wish any ill on anybody. The codefendant, I didn't want him to get shot. And the district attorney, I hope she rests in peace; I wish the best for her family and everyone who grieves her loss. Re-fucking-gardless, we need to pay for what we do in this life. Karma is a mirror.

KARMIC DEBT

Honestly, you don't need to be a firm believer in the laws that the government puts on you. You don't even need to believe that drugs are bad for you, but the fact is you do need to pay attention to laws of the universe, like karma. You can't push weight and think that by causing such drama on someone else's family, causing someone else's kids to get hooked on dope, that it's not going to come back around to you. If you push dope to someone else's kids, chances are someone's going to push it back to yours—and here the cycle begins.

We are consistently punished by the
universe for our negative actions.

We are consistently punished by the universe for our negative actions. We're punished with time. The amount of shit that I did wrong caused me to be punished with ten years of time because I did so many violent acts toward people and brought so much pain and negativity into their lives. I caused so many problems with my lust for money that I was building up karmic debt, which was only resolved by me having to sit down for that time and experience the pain that I inflicted on everybody else. The universe punishes you with time for your negative acts.

Try this. It's an eye for an eye. Next time you get into an argument with someone, you treat them like shit. Just watch how they're on your mind for the next thirty minutes to three hours—whatever it may be. It's always according to how brutal you were in the conversation. And in my case, I was particularly brutal, particularly violent toward people. My time and my pain were extreme. One day, about seven years into my sentence, I finally realized when my karmic debt was paid up and everything just became clear. Karmic debt blocks your intuition and keeps you from manifesting your ultimate vision.

We're granted time by the universe when we act in a positive manner. Too many fucking people try to act like they're not doing anything wrong. When I see someone consistently being held back and they can just never seem to get ahead, I just ask them, "What the fuck are you doing? What are you doing?" Usually, it's completely obvious where they're fucking up and where they're building up this karmic debt. But sometimes it's not so obvious.

You always need to question people who can't seem to get ahead because they're doing something. It could be something as simple as negative thoughts. It could just be a negative attitude. It could be fucking shit they've said before, shitting on people, treating people like shit, and this is holding them back from getting ahead. When you truly give what you want in return, you will propel yourself forward so fucking quickly. It's crazy.

I see people in the pen all the time, and at one point I was talking to a particular inmate, Evil from Compton. He was dating a correctional officer while dealing dope inside, and he was killing it. I mean, he was buying houses out of state and buying cars for his chick. He made his apparent "success" known every day in that he always had shit for making $20 spreads (meaning his meals). Inmates are usually saving up for a $5 sausage and some ramen noodles, while he was eating what is considered baller in prison on the fucking regular.

He always had phones on hand and anything else he needed to keep playing his games. He was absolutely slaughtering it. As I was really in tune with myself and the laws of the universe, I just fucking knew it was a matter of time before it all caught up to him as it caught up to me and basically everyone I had ever known. One day, after he received a Saran-wrapped batch of dope, he was raided by some of the guards. After he tried swallowing the whole load, he ended up choking to death in the dayroom as the entire building watched.

This shit ain't nothing fucking new. You guys know this. Nobody wins in that game.

One of my exes still sold heroin and shit, still fucked around when she got out. She swore up and fucking down that she didn't use it. I told her, "No, fuck that. You're fucking up someone's kid."

And she's like, "No, that's an adult. He's thirty-five …."

I said, "That's somebody's son. My brother's addicted to drugs. He's in and out the pen all the time. I see the pain it causes my mom. When you know this is the truth happening around you, how can you be part of the problem and think you're not going to pay!?"

If a man is right, his world will be right.

That's just horrible character. We can never act in this manner if we think we're going to live a positive life. Positive thoughts and positive actions lead to a positive life: it's that simple. If a man is right, his world will be right. I'm a living testament to that. Fact is *you* know what's wrong. We all do! Because every vice has an excuse attached, an excuse ready at the tongue. We should never ever think that by bringing someone else down we can elevate ourselves, but the lust for possessions in this life has made so many very careless.

The pen is full of that shit. People are selling out their own people just to have extra soups in their locker. And out here, people are throwing other people's lives away just to get a new Benz on the street. It's fucking bullshit. It's something we need to quit glorifying. I'm telling you, I did it the right way this time. I brought everybody else up with me.

There are two ways to exercise strength in this fucking life: (1) pushing down, and (2) lifting up. If we lift each other up, we will get much further. I'm using this tactic now, but when I was on the extreme other end of the spectrum I was using the push-down tactic, the forceful tactic—being a fucking weak-ass motherfucker and using fucking violence on people, holding them down by enabling their addictions for my own personal gain: the epitome of bitch behavior.

Now I'm living life the right way and it's working out for me tenfold. It's working out for everybody around me as well because I personify the teaching at a high degree, so others wish to learn. I never need to look over my shoulder anymore. I mean, imagine that! Do you actually fucking think you'll get away with taking someone's life just to fucking fill your bank account? Let's say, during a robbery you shoot someone, or you sell some dope to someone and they shoot it up; then they straight peace-the-fuck-out and overdose. That happens all too often and motherfuckers forget karma is a mirror. We get what we give. Hope you're ready.

Going to the penitentiary is like the circle of life. When you enter the pen, you have nothing and all you want is the most basic of human needs. You're stripped down to bare essentials (what we refer to as "state issue"), so you can see everything for what it really is. You have nothing. So, all you want is more food and yard. You're just simply at the fucking bottom so you just need necessities and you'll be happy, or should I say content? I don't believe in happiness.

Now, once you get those, here starts the perpetual pleasure-chasing that ruins lives when we fail to moderate. Everybody around you has nice shoes, they have coffee, and they have a TV. Now we're automatically drawn to wanting that, like it's going to fulfill us in some form or fashion when, in all reality, as humans we possess everything inside us to create how we feel about and view our surroundings. That materialistic shit does nothing.

Always, always, always remember your worst of times.

Once we've elevated to getting our TV, our coffee, this and that, here comes the perpetual pleasure-seeking. Next, we travel outside the fence and want our people to visit all the time; when we get that, it's simply not good enough. We see friends and family a few times, and then, just by our own fucking inability to recognize that this could be the last day we see them, we want more. We want to be with them on the street. We want to get back to our old life, which is not a possibility for a long time, if ever, for most.

When inmates get back to the street, many of them fall right back into drug use. They don't even see their loved ones around them; they just have a singular focus on their selfish desires because they failed to stop the perpetual pleasure-chasing cycle that started back in the pen. The very people they were crying about before, they treat horribly and take for granted. This is those fake-hard fraudulent-ass motherfuckers who cry about their kids in the pen and then they get back out and run straight back to the needle because they're soft-ass bitches, straight-up.

Our job on this planet is to heal our trauma, eventually assisting in the cycle being broken.

Always, always, always remember your worst of times. That's why I share my stories. Any stupid motherfucker who even lets the thought materialize, "Oh, move past the prison shit ...." Fuck you! Straight-up, remembering your worst of times in your best of times keeps you grateful. I don't even show people the levels of success I've attained, because it means nothing to me. I show them the level of success that I've brought unto others because that means everything to me. A life worth living is a life lived for other people, and keeping others out of the penitentiary—somewhere that caused me massive amounts of pain, as you can fucking tell—means everything to me. Our job on this planet is to heal our trauma—heal what caused us the most pain our entire lives and pay that wisdom forward—eventually assisting in the cycle being broken.

WINNER MINDSET

The way to overcome everything is to learn the mindset where you look at everything as a win. The obstacles are the path. The path is supplied in overcoming those obstacles. Your character is created through the obstacles you thought you could never hurdle. When I was on these massive lockdowns in prison we wouldn't leave our cells for months. During these times I saw every undesirable condition I faced full of strength and a grateful heart as a win.

On October 11, 2011, in Sayre, Oklahoma, at a CCA facility that housed all California inmates, a riot broke out with over 400 inmates stabbing and beating each other for hours on end. This massive riot ended with everyone on a racially based lockdown that lasted an entire year, an entire fucking year without stepping one foot out of your cell. Finding the strength to rise every morning at 2:45 AM in these conditions was just seen as psychotic by most. I saw it as my first win of the day, and it gave me the pride and momentum to go straight into my workout.

By moving straight onto a win of your choice first thing in the morning, you're leaving nothing up to chance. This is how you truly construct the unbreakable mind.

Once I got that second win, I had built the strength and discipline to eat only the food that served my purpose from the trays we were given. My purpose was self-mastery, and the key to self-mastery is through what we ingest. So, through this process I taught myself to find enjoyment from the struggle and build a level of mental fortitude that is today my most valued asset.

By moving straight onto a win of your choice first thing in the morning, you're leaving nothing up to chance. This is how you truly construct the unbreakable mind. You fucking move straight from something that was a perceived loss, like losing freedom, straight to a huge fucking win like self-mastery in any situation. For a motherfucker like me, when I'm going after a goal, the second my internal dialogue goes south, goes negative, I pivot, moving straight to the next area that demands attention.

I never exist in the losing or victim mindset for more than a fraction of a second. I refer to that as *closing the window*. I see all negative feelings or mental states simply as a notification for self-preservation. I know I can't exist in that losing frame of mind for even a second if I want to work at my top level. That negative downturn in feeling or thought was simply a notification to keep moving forward, a nudge from the universe to step out of that anxious state we all exist in too often, back into flow state where we're most powerful.

Your obstacles are the compass rose, directing you down the path to where your weakness lies. You must *laser focus* on your weaknesses to level the fuck up. I don't give a fuck about your strengths. So many live life based on standing so proudly upon their strengths, magnifying their accolades and never extinguishing their true weaknesses. Why would you keep applying pressure to what's already working? That's improper energy allocation. Magnify those weaknesses. Extinguish them. Watch how much clearer your conscience gets. It's not just for you; it's for others. You're helping by not passing the pain—from your true deficiencies—down the line to your children or any of your people.

Nobody gives a shit about your Rolls-Royce if you got titties, motherfucker.

Think about that shot-out motherfucker who's got way too much money. I always talk about these motherfuckers because I see them from so far away, like "Hey! Look at my Rolls-Royce! Look at my D cup! Check out how I obviously let myself go!" If that's your ambition, know this: nobody gives a shit about your Rolls-Royce if you got titties, motherfucker. Nobody. You will draw in all the wrong people with that bullshit. What you validate yourself with deep in your heart, others will want from you. So if you lead with materials over character, don't be surprised when you poison your circle.

PICK A SIDE

Stay present during the pain. If you're an athlete, when you're injured, that's painful. When you're in prison and you're injured, you're fucking fighting for your life to build muscles so that when that shit cracks you don't end up a corpse. It's war in there. It's fucking painful knowing that you could be the liability. But the thing is, when it comes to your pain, I don't give a fuck. Anytime you're faced with adversity, know that during all times of adversity there is a simultaneous seed planted for the virtue of its matching.

For however deep that adversity was, if you overcome it, you have that exact amount of virtue. Why? Because that was your weak point and when you overcame it, your mindset was forever changed. Your mindset was forever changed because you knew that was your weakness and you leveled up by choice—through conscious endeavor.

The real fucking ones who need real accountability, who need hard truth, are stubborn and strong. They need someone to fucking hit them in the fucking face with that shit. That's what the fuck I did to myself. I would never fucking give you anything other than what worked for me. I won't tone it down.

And you're not my people if you need me to tone it down. We know our vibe attracts our tribe; energy exchange is the language of the universe.

You can either be a real man who lives in a conscious-congruent manner, or you can be the fake-hard motherfucker who lives completely out of alignment with his authentic self. The fake-hard motherfucker with face tats, riddled with vices, physically soft, placating pleasure at every turn—this man lets himself and his family down by choosing the easiest route to make money and live life. Prison is plagued with fake-hards. The streets are plagued with them. It's the costume party where you look tough, you look hard, but you live in the exact opposite manner. You live physically soft. You do not work hard. You have no character. Everything you do is incongruent with your conscience and the universal laws that I teach.

Universal laws are what govern us. These individuals so out of alignment are the ones who truly know the answer. What's that, Wes? Yes, they fucking know the answer. They know they don't want to be on drugs. They know they want to make their families proud. They know they want to be physically in good shape. How-fucking-ever, they choose not to out of pure weakness. Fake-hards are the weakest individuals. They focus on their strengths, they ignore their obstacles, and they live an incongruent life.

You can continue a life plagued with incongruences, or you can just be removed from the yard.

If you're feeling like I might be describing you, then pick a side. Pick a fucking side. You can continue a life plagued with incongruences, or you can just be removed from the yard. There's a new man out there. He's fucking obsessed with success through personal development. He's fucking savage in all endeavors. He's ready for anything and he's got a huge fucking heart. He believes in karmic debt; he treats people with respect and he gives the energy he wants in return.

This energy I'm providing is to fuel you. It's to create the habits on the other side of your weaknesses to make you strong in the areas you're weak. You don't need to be like me. I don't want you to be like me. I don't want you to have my answers. I want you to find your own.

You're going to find your answers the second you tap in by going as hard as you fucking can in every area—mind, body, and soul. Intense, painful reflection. Intense, painful workouts. And intense, savage fucking diets that leave you hungry. I want you fucking hungry, physically and mentally. When we're hungry, we fucking fight.

3

TRUE PURPOSE

(Simplifying the Path to Your Genius)

The process, the process, the process. This is living in the moment. And right now is the moment. You must train your mind to operate from your mental witness. This means standing back and knowing you're not the thoughts you're having, you're not these fucking desires. You're none of that. You're the person who stands back and watches your mind work. That's you. You're in control. As a strong mental witness, you can check these desires you have, these choices you're about to make, and ensure they are directly in line with the future you're creating. You're in control of this. Stand back, watch it work. Motherfucking flow state. This is the moment.

Personally, I only see the principles and the character it took to achieve the goal. I don't even care about the goal itself. I love when someone is looking in the mirror and they're proud of their results. I know what it took. Now, the superficial simple fucks expose themselves because the way we view the world is simply a confession of character. They only see the short route that must have been taken; they don't understand what it takes.

Don't you ever forget for one second, not one fucking second, that the only way I identified this shit, the only way I figured all this out, was by facing that man in the accountability mirror. When I stood in that mirror and I said, "You're being a fucking bitch, Wes," that's when I was able to change it. What we're doing here is enlightenment at the highest degree. This is how we change everything: by always pointing the finger at ourselves so we are in control, opposed to living in that victim mindset. If we change our habits, thoughts, and actions, this is the only way we can change our lives. And, as far as I know, there's not one person who doesn't want to enhance their lives in some form or fashion. So, we work to become, NOT acquire.

Anything I share that's seemingly negative, if it fits you and it stings, GOOD. The best part about all this shit is that when we identify it, we can change it. So let it sting, bitch. Then *put the fucking work in.* Everybody starts off craving the result, but as you stick to the process over time you mature with the process, and you realize it's much deeper. You realize it's about how you feel. Everything in this life is about how we feel. How we feel shapes our perspective on life in any endeavor we're pursuing.

One of the fakest fake-hards you'll come across in this life is the person who quits when they're after a certain goal that their heart desires, the superficial fuck who's only after the results. If you were ever fucking after some physique goals or financial goals, and so on, and you fucking quit, it's because you're a superficial fuck and you only wanted the result. Period.

We chase the feeling working out gives us internally, and our exterior is a byproduct.

You didn't want the process. You're not present, not existing in flow state, not being and becoming—so you're not in your optimal state of complete focus. The crazy thing about fitness is that people who quit always point to a person who actually gets massive results in fitness as being the superficial person.

To them I say, "Guess what, motherfucker! Your perception of me is a reflection of you, motherfucker. And you don't get it." We chase the feeling working out gives us internally, and our exterior is a byproduct. Quitters chase the results, which never come fast enough, so they fucking tap on their goals.

ALIGNING PRINCIPLES & CHARACTER

Your conscience is the guide to being
in complete alignment.

When you're in complete alignment with your authentic self, you will attract everything you desire in life. The universe bends for those who truly listen to the path being supplied. As I've been explaining, your conscience is the guide to being in complete alignment. I call it conscience-congruency.

We are being led. The steps we are being called upon to take moment by moment throughout our days are being supplied to us by our conscience. My path led to the penitentiary from refusal to adhere to the call of my conscience and ultimately to where I am today. God, the universe—whatever your religious beliefs—one thing is for sure: our conscience is the authentic voice of our creator. Take it as such and your life will drastically change.

The mistakes that pulled and pushed me out of alignment came down to my attempts at making money too quickly, illegally. I needed to realize that I was literally not creating the person I saw in my head. I was not in alignment with the vision I had for self. So physically, mentally, and spiritually, I was completely not adhering to the path being supplied by my conscience, which would have created my optimal self. I like to refer to our conscience's voice as the call from our higher self, who we will become if we adhere to the steps that our conscience is giving.

Our conscience is the authentic voice of our creator.

Now, our conscience is creating that vision of self, what we see when we see us at our optimal potential. When we wake up in the morning, when we walk in front of the mirror, our conscience asks us to quit eating so much or to start fucking working out harder. These insights, as harsh as they might feel, are the steps that we must take when our highest self is pulling us up to make drastic changes in our behavior. It's character construction. And it's paramount to not blocking yourself from being in alignment with your true self.

Let's keep it simple. We need to simplify our lives. For me, the main goal that I wake up with every morning is to never break character. When we break character, it kicks us completely out of alignment. We are not in flow state. We are not living in the moment. When we break character, we are automatically attached to the past event in which we broke character; next, karmic debt ensues. This takes us out of alignment and keeps us from adhering to our vision and our path.

It's so foolish that everybody wants their path to be lit from beginning to end before they start to walk it. The fact is, by answering the call from your conscience, moment by moment, the path is lit, step by step. Faith has always been a prerequisite in order to live a life of purpose. Your plans at your current state of consciousness will always limit you. Instead, just BE and watch all develop around this rare human of your creation from simply living in a purpose-over-pleasure manner.

OUR TRUE PURPOSE
(LIGHTING THE PATH TO ALIGNMENT)

When you get your first paycheck at fourteen years old, thirteen years old, you do not think about amassing generational wealth. It starts off superficial. It starts off selfish. You just want to buy yourself something. So, for every endeavor we pursue, our path will start off like this. My path started off superficial as fuck; I wanted to be buff and look a certain way, and I wanted to make myself feel good. And, hey, that doesn't mean that you're incorrect for starting like that; it means that you're at the beginning of a path. The beginning of everything starts off juvenile in form and then matures throughout the length of the term of the path you're taking.

In terms of the path I want you to take, for the purposes of this book, it's aligned with these principles:

1. Purpose over pleasure
2. Acquire what you admire
3. Habitual construction
4. Power of gratitude
5. Personify the teaching

I started off wanting to just create a certain body, a certain look, so that I was one of the hardest motherfuckers on the hardest prison yards. Through pure fucking physical presence and conduct, I would secure my spot as a leader in the most vicious California prisons. As I was developing my external aesthetics, I was just called to my higher purpose through self-help books that I was gravitating toward while on my own personal development journey. I kept finding the sting through poignant-as-fuck quotes. Quotes are known as the wisdom of the ages, and they struck me as such. My vision began getting very clear as I saw myself constructing and evolving.

So, I started off just wanting to be swole—superficial as fuck—but that graduated into working out for life, knowing that it does something for me. It:

- Raises my rate of vibration

- Creates a high level of PMA (which is a positive mental attitude)

- Aligns me with the day

- Puts me on a great path mentally

Today, my credo is that life happens for me.
So anytime adversity strikes, I know life is
happening for me and I use it for my benefit.

Later down the road, as I started picking up quote books, I found myself consuming the wisdom of the ages from Albert Einstein to Marcus Aurelius. I was just consuming quotes and writing them out in my own words. I wasn't just understanding them, and I wasn't just being a motivation consumer; I was truly living these quotes, embodying them, and applying them to my life across the board.

Today, my credo is that life happens for me. So anytime adversity strikes, I know life is happening for me and I use it for my benefit. I've coupled this concept with "The way you do anything is the way you do everything," and I've let both run me through life in a positive manner. If anything negative happens, I have these fail-safes, these gems, to negate any negative mindset that I would face.

The path begins in a juvenile fashion. Then we start to become wiser, and the path evolves based on wisdom, mental clarity, and focus. Purpose over fucking pleasure overrides the superficiality of it, and the true reason, our "why" behind the goal, takes over. This is solidified through habitual construction.

Through proper mental programming, we construct who we are in our mind.

In the penitentiary, there's massive politics for each race. If you're white, you're going to listen to your people. These are massive politics, and anytime your people ask you anything, the answer is "Yes." There's a mandatory wake-up time, a mandatory workout, and unfortunately a lot of mandatory violence that comes as part of being in your prison gang. If you're white in California, you're in a prison gang. This seems massively negative, and it is—if you don't see the silver lining to it. The silver lining to for me was that this way of conducting myself completely rewired my subconscious. I reprogrammed my mind to be so structured, so militant, that I will never give up on a goal once it's in my sight.

Through proper mental programming, we construct who we are in our mind. By reading quotes and affirmations and consistently applying them, we are constructing our core beliefs behind the words that resonate with us. After we construct who we are mentally, and through our physical acts, we automatically become someone who can't help but wake up at a certain time, never miss a workout, and stay in alignment with our higher self. Habitually, we're creating someone, mind, body, and soul, who's pushing themselves to the highest degree at all times.

A lot of people use the wrong emotions while they're constructing the individual they wish to be. Intention is everything. If we construct an individual with the incorrect emotions, we get the incorrect outcome. And to this end, the power of gratitude is everything. When we operate out of love over hate, then the intention and outcome are completely different. When we're grateful for our life, when we love our life—and this is why we conduct ourselves in the manner we conduct ourselves in—we get a completely opposite outcome than if we're doing it in spite of people.

Gratitude kicks down the mother-
fucking door to higher intelligence.

The dumbest thing I've ever heard is when people say, "I'm going to show all my haters by becoming so successful," or "Success is the greatest revenge." These are the stupidest forms of motivation. These are the subpar forms of mindset construction because the root of them is not love.

When you wake up grateful for your life, you love your life. You're in a grateful state, and gratitude kicks down the motherfucking door to higher intelligence. Once *you* are tapped into infinite intelligence you will see that you're simply an outward flow of wisdom and confidence by simply being.

I use the power of gratitude to hold myself to my daily tasks. That was always the vision I had, sitting on my rack in the morning, drinking my coffee in tears, because I had such a clear vision of my future family. It was so clear to me how my wife would view me when I had put in ten years of painful workouts and an intense study into the wisdom of the ages to construct an individual capable of being the husband she needed, the father my son needed—a quality example, physically, mentally, and spiritually. This vision of what would come to be when I stuck to the path was my guiding light.

Purpose, admiration, habit construction, and gratitude. The jacked up, buff jackass that my younger self desired to become took a back fucking seat. My principles and actions aligned with my future until finally, further down the road as I matured, I started to teach others. I reached the point where I came up with what I call our life's purpose.

If you're not "it," then bow the fuck out and
come back when you realign yourself.

I believe our life's purpose is to create the individual we admire in every way so that we can just give that individual to the world. If you look at my path to alignment, I went from superficially creating the body I wanted to consuming wisdom from all the top fucking philosophers of the ages. And then I dove into combining that wisdom and that look that I created to teach others to be better people.

My point is that I needed to personify the teaching. For others around us to wish to learn, we must personify the teaching, and that's what I knew I had to do to get through to the people around me. So many messages are lost due to leaders not strictly following their own teachings. Hypothetical is hypocritical, and that goes moment by moment. If you're not "it" (meaning truly embodying your teachings), then bow the fuck out and come back when you realign yourself.

There is nothing greater on this planet than the feeling of when you have a broken individual, which I once was, and you take them under your wing and you give them power again. You give them the meaning of life again, and then you help heal them through this same process. My experience is why I know that true alignment exists, because I went from being the worst motherfucker I know to where I'm at today by just aligning myself with quality character and following the path that my conscience was supplying to me. And that path was in alignment with my universal vision.

YOUR VISION

Follow your dreams. Follow your vision. Don't listen to anybody who's telling you otherwise. It's your genius. It's supplied to you from above. The universe has given you a hookup. You have the complete guideline at your fingertips.

Ten years ago in the penitentiary, I had the same vision I have today, and I just kept pushing. I saw it so clearly. There was nothing else. I was going to get blasted. I was going to get swole. And I was going to live a lifestyle that I wanted, using social media to inspire people. I would use these platforms to help people. That's the true purpose, and no other road would be accepted.

The universe has given you a hookup. You have the complete guideline at your fingertips.

I don't look any different from going to the gym every day now. I won't all of a sudden just build 20 more pounds of muscle. Nothing like that's going to happen to me. So why do I go? Why do I go every day now? It's a deeper reason. Stacking those wins makes me feel great from within. I have a different energy. Everyone around me feels it. It pushes them.

When you see the people around you succeed, it's tenfold what it means to you when you hit your own goals. You'll always be you, no matter where you're at. It don't fucking matter if you're ripped. You're used to it. You grew into that. You've matured to that level of physique. You've matured to that level of money that you have. You've matured to know who you are internally. Life will never be that different, being you at any area of time, unless you master the day and learn that what we're all truly after is inner peace, to just feel content at all times in knowing this is under your control. Life and how we feel is a matter of perspective. In the SHU, I've had the greatest days internally that I've ever known, with nothing, and some of the worst in my penthouse purely due to perspective.

When you see the people around you
succeed, it's tenfold what it means to
you when you hit your own goals.

I always told everyone in the penitentiary, "I'm going to be a trainer. I'm going to coach people online. I'm going to use Instagram. I'm going to use these platforms." And they always told me, "I'm going to be a trainer too. I'm going to be a personal trainer." But I could tell from their actions, habits, and overall interest that they wouldn't.

Everybody saw me training other inmates in prison, so there was no doubt when I shared my vision that I would continue. Motherfuckers don't get it. Become valuable and let success be the byproduct; never simply chase success.

It was a win to me just to make you feel like a
bitch. My character was so fucking wrong.

Ultimately, don't wait, and don't follow paths you've been told by others you're supposed to follow. Follow your vision. And when you reach the point where you need to personify the teaching, don't let yourself feel any guilt about creating a service. Provide a service that was life-changing to you and collect a fee, provide exponential worth. I get told every day online and in person, "Wes, you saved my life," or, "Man, you changed my life," and I'm like, "I know ...." I changed mine with this same process.

Following my vision changed my life. There is no denying it. I was the fucking worst. I would have smoked your ass over ten grand, or even fucking five grand. I would've smoked you over a fucking disagreement. I didn't care about karmic debt. I didn't care about these wins. It was a win to me just to make you feel like a bitch. My character was so fucking wrong.

By now, I've flipped my way of thinking completely, because I've become accountable. I can help you become accountable through what I share. And everything I share is about following your dreams. It has nothing to do with the direct societal path everyone tells you, "Well, you just go to school for eight years. You become a doctor and your life's perfect." I know plenty of doctors whose lives aren't perfect because they don't seek within. They don't find their answers. They don't unlock and experience these breakthroughs mentally.

You need these breakthroughs. You need to go through this morning reflection process. Every day is a new one and you must earn confidence daily. You need to earn your answers daily. You need to reassure yourself with action; confidence is simply a byproduct of consistent implementation. People sometimes say, "Wes, you're ripped. I don't believe that you aren't always confident."

Trust me, if I don't earn it today, I feel like the fat little fourteen-year-old I was growing up. If I don't earn it today, I regress right to that state because we cannot lie to ourselves. Each day truly is new. So don't ever mistake anything other than your daily process as building you from within. You build yourself from within, and the energy flows outward.

In the pen everybody would say, "I'm going to be this. I'm going to be that," but it's motherfucking action. I've said it before. Vision with no action is fucking delusion. You can just start working toward your dreams right now. Today. You can just take the path that nobody else takes and just figure it out along the way. If you never quit, you'll always fill in the blanks. You'll always find the answers.

Simply put, imperfect action is the secret. When I got out, I didn't have a training app. I just knew how to track macros and get swole. And then I started using Instagram. I fucking started posting all my shit, everything I was doing, all the steps, learning as I went and sharing what was most personal to me about the journey.

Personal development is always the beginning.

It's so simple. If you just share what works for you and you have some results in any area of life, you can provide a service around it and become a business. Don't fucking put all these fake-ass things in your mind that don't suit your optimal outcome. Simply seek to provide worth to people's lives and they're grateful.

Don't even think about providing a service and collecting a profit. Provide worth to individuals' lives through what was valuable to you. On your own, if you haven't built self-worth, respect, and confidence for self, well then ... until you heal yourself, you cannot heal other people. So, personal development is always the beginning.

Get the fuck after it, today. Start learning, start comprehending, and start applying. If everything seems too fucking mismatched from all the information out there about training and nutrition, hire a coach. A coach can give you that direct line of sight, right to where you want to go quickly. Like, I don't know how to do anything to my car; I need to get a mechanic because I'm not about to spend the next six fucking months trying to figure out how to work on my vehicle. It's foolish.

Anything that generates flow state to you is a direct line to where you should be working.

Find your zone of genius. Find your area of expertise and just kill it at that. Master that. Don't be that fucking jack-of-all-trades, master of none. We find what works for us in flow state. That's fucking right. Flow state. Flow state. Flow state. I always fell into flow state during a workingout.

When I work out, I don't notice time as it passes. That is the definition of inner peace—when time passes and we don't notice. Anything that generates flow state to you is a direct line to where you should be working. And you should be able to generate flow state in the three main areas: mind, body, and soul.

Flow state is when you're just locked in like nothing can stop you. I used to enter this zone while sitting on my rack reading in the penitentiary for hours, just researching training and nutrition. Boom, boom, boom! Studying and trying to find answers. Boom, boom, boom! Looking for different answers. Boom! Driven by urgency. You need that intensity. You need that desire.

I found most of my knowledge through trial and error and reading my limited resources while in the penitentiary. The internet has leveled the playing field. If you don't fucking know something, "Google it, Homie." Google that fucking shit and apply it! The whole world is at your fingertips. Get your desired results in yourself, then pay it fucking forward. A life lived for others is truly a life worth living.

4

FUCKING ABIDE!

(Purpose Over Pleasure)

If there's one thing I strive to personify in this life, it's my favorite quote, "Purpose over pleasure." We tie up all loose ends simultaneously if we live in this manner. By consistently choosing purposeful acts over pleasurable ones throughout our days, we rewire the landscape of our minds. I've reached a point where pleasure-seeking is painful. It's fucking painful because I know I'm stepping further and further away from my true goals.

I draw the line at a 90/10 ratio: 90 percent purpose-driven, 10 percent pleasure. This will get you everywhere you want to go. Think about it. The motherfuckers who win in this life live based on their commitment, not their feelings. When we're chasing pleasure, it's because were caving to our selfish desires that do nothing to help build us up.

Fuck that. That won't get you anywhere and is the main reason so many live lives of steady regression. The low is always going to match the high you get when you chase pleasure.

Perpetual pleasure-chasing is the end to most people because there is no actual end. They're lost. They have no more purpose. Stop fucking looking externally for the path you're supposed to take with your life. It's only supplied by your conscience. Every little step your conscience is telling you to take is your path.

The motherfuckers who win in this life live based on their commitment, not their feelings.

Most motherfuckers are trying to create a vision years down the road. Yes, we have long view. But we choose to stack small wins daily like clockwork. This is how we master each day. As we know, we never rise to our goals, we fall to the strength of our system.

The way we choose to conduct ourselves each day is our system of creation, internally and externally. That's how we gain control. That's how we habitually construct the individual who can withstand anything. At this moment we're walking in line with our conscience. We're not getting too far in the future and we're not fucking dwelling on the past. Every little fucking step your conscience tells you to do is creating who you fucking are, keeping you aligned with your life purpose.

If it tells you to open the door and wait for that person, then wait and do it. You're creating better character. If it tells you to get the fuck up and exercise, then get up and do it because it's making you a quality example for those around you—to be healthier, to seek confidence, to earn what they fucking want for themselves.

This way you see me fucking speak—the words you're reading right fucking now—this program of stacking small daily wins, I'm living it. I've been doing this forever. It's just now coming out. Life is not about sprinting to our goals, it's about moderating desire and the men we become through the process. If we fucking moderate desires—and we learn to gain pleasure from the sacrifices we make—we can use enough delayed gratification to acquire what we wish, and more importantly create who we unbiasedly admire.

Every little fucking step your conscience tells you to do is creating who you fucking are, keeping you aligned with your life's purpose.

You're getting in your own way; it's as simple as that. You could be as ripped as you want and as rich as you want with everything you currently have—if you got the fuck out of your own way and solely sought purpose. Funny thing is, at first there is friction but once your mindset shifts the sacrifices, your ability to go without becomes your pleasure. Everybody's fucking trading what they ultimately desire—in their heart, for themselves, and their people—for what they want right now. Instant gratification is a straight-up disease. The realest fact is that getting what you want is riches, but being able to go without—now, that's power. Seek power.

The other day I saw a post that freaked me the fuck out. This seemingly productive dude was like, "Well, I'm really successful. I get most of my work done at night, but I know I should get up earlier. I kind of regret not doing that." And it just fucked me up.

Me personally? I know regret is our guideline. There is no other reason we're feeling like that. That is our conscience telling us to change something—and it's okay. He was doing good. He remains successful. But he's fucking blind for not noticing that getting up earlier is his level-up. Honestly, extinguishing all regret is your next level, because energy is our most valuable resource—*not* time, as most believe—and that loss of focus due to his regret is a massive energy leak. When we remove what we regret in this fucking life, that's how we level the fuck up. We can zero in on everything more by focusing on what we shouldn't do, instead of on what we should.

The problem is *everyone* is always trying to add shit to their lives instead of following this rule, the simple guidance of regret. "Hey, Wes, should I add cardio to my training and fucking diet?" Fuck the fucking cardio for now, motherfucker. Quit eating whole fucking Little Debbie's boxes on your cheat days—okay? You can't add cardio to Little Debbie's and start killing it. Like, what the fuck is that?

As I've shared before, stagnation does not exist. We're either growing or we're dying. We're either progressing or regressing. And the fucking fact is that if we're not forcing ourselves to level up, we will feel—simply by contrast—like we're not living up to our potential. This will lead to lack of confidence, which will lead to these other problems. Which will lead to us feeling like we're not fucking progressing. Which means we feel like we're dying.

When we remove what we regret in this fucking life, that's how we level the fuck up.

So, this is where all the fucking problems sneak in. If we're not proud of ourselves—if we're not progressing, if we're not forcing ourselves to evolve—then we're dying inside. Wake the fuck up today. Listen to your conscience and walk directly in line with it. If it tells your fucking chunky ass to get to the gym, then go. If it tells you to limit them fucking Little Debbie's and not have that fucking extra muffin with your coffee, then fucking do it. Your conscience will never sell you out. The conscience is known as the only incorruptible thing about us. Walk in line with it. Conscience-congruency. It's simple. You know the answers. We all do. They have, and will always, lie within.

SELF-INFLICTED ADVERSITY

As you should know from my Introduction, I grew up in San Diego. I was all about smoking weed, skating, snowboarding, surfing, and selling weed. I wanted the easy life, to just lie back and chill. As many of us think when we're younger what life is all about, I thought the definition of success was that you don't have to do much. I watched gangster movies and they would always glorify the easy life. I saw that pleasure was what hood life was about. Young and immature, I thought pleasure was the purpose.

My perpetual pleasure-chasing just led to a life of not being fulfilled. Was that the end of it? Fuck no. I would just consistently chase it more—more easy money, and more and more highs that had the equivalent lows because I was just always seeking pleasure. This was an endless battle of pleasure-chasing that we all conduct ourselves in—if we don't learn to limit pleasure.

My chase led me to the penitentiary. It was a downward spiral. I would consistently just look for a new high. I would try to get money quicker. And all these ways of living just landed me behind bars quicker than the money came in. Once I was in the pen, I started seeing flaws in the pleasure-based lifestyle. So I went deep within. And I started validating myself with my true character and finding my purpose. As you might fuckin' guess, that's where I adopted the mindset of purpose over pleasure.

Living a purpose-over-pleasure-based lifestyle is a win-win. We win on both ends. First off, we're building ourselves without taking anything away—so we end up living in the present, chasing the feeling daily of being a quality individual and getting that result daily, which ultimately leads to the completion of the long-term goals we have, as well, at the highest level. We're after that purpose of feeling good, never living with regret, and never having these massive lows that are attached to pleasure-seeking.

In the penitentiary, sitting in my cell, reflecting, it was easy to see the flaws in my pleasure-seeking past. Mentally, I started to actually couple pleasure with regression. And I'm a progressive individual; I like to move forward really quickly with my goals. So, anything that fell into the pleasure-seeking category—sleeping in, food that was out of alignment with my goals, or not training my hardest—brought me further away from my actual goal. And that became more uncomfortable than the work I fucking had to do in order to accomplish my lofty goals. I could tell it was not aligned with the vision I was creating for myself; discomfort ultimately became my comfort zone, as progression was my ultimate desire.

Even though you're in the penitentiary, regardless of what you might think, there's a number of ways that people can seek pleasure. I mean, just the eating of junk food all day. The only real, legal high that people can get in prison is snacks and foods. So they would seek instant gratification and pleasure through "meals" that were massively unhealthy for them. And thus they were digging themselves deeper into this massive hole of pleasure-chasing to where they ended up just distorting their whole vision of self, which leads to a lack of confidence and ultimately self-hatred.

For some, this meant a hard turn toward vices. They went toward drug use and alcohol—and we know how that bitch-ass shit ends up. They would just bring themselves down deeper and deeper into that hole of despair.

Discomfort ultimately became my comfort zone,
as progression was my ultimate desire.

In learning to sacrifice when we operate out of pure purpose, this is how we avoid sabotaging ourselves. We create a vision of self that knows we are worthy of our vision. This is how we end up getting our massive goals in both aspects. In the culmination of all this, I began to take pleasure in not being pleased.

I remember certain events in massive lockdowns. I went more than a year without stepping out of a prison cell—not one foot—when I would watch the other inmates in the building losing it mentally. I was in the SHU (segregated housing unit), feeling the energy. I could feel people cracking, just losing their minds, not being able to deal with the extreme isolation. In that moment my purpose of getting out, being a better man, would just drive me. I would absorb their loss of power, loss of control. They were limiting themselves with so many desires, and my only desire was to maintain my purpose of creating pleasure through my daily process.

Basically, at a certain point of growth you learn to take pride in not being pleased. You learn to get pleasure from not getting your way. This is the optimal state of growth, where you learn to find your pleasure in not getting your way, which in turn causes you to progress the most. Your progression, in the end, is the byproduct of sticking to your goals, as confidence in all areas is a byproduct of consistent implementation.

I would find pleasure in my ability to stick to an extremely structured program. I would find the utmost pleasure and validation through my ability to wake up at the same time every morning—2:45 AM, whether I wanted to or not—and go straight into my personal growth process where I would reflect. I would conduct myself with a high level of introspection and I would read books that resonated with me. The books raised my rate of vibration, my frequency, and just caused a type of contentment and internal peace that most people will never know because they're consistently pleasure-chasing. Then I would go directly into my workout. I was on a mission and I had found what I call Life's Purpose ....

To create the man we admire in all ways so that we can just give him away.

Your progression, in the end, is the byproduct of sticking to your goals, as confidence in all areas is a byproduct of consistent implementation.

To do this we must inflict adversity upon ourselves. This is the "new age" way of doing what cultures have done since the dawn of time. To find yourself, you need to find inner peace and contentment. Ancient cultures practiced fasting, extreme treks, and seeking isolation. I essentially found myself doing just that in a modern-day version. So, again, I thank the California Department of Corrections and Rehabilitation (CDCR) system.

Thank you CDCR for putting me in extreme isolation. Thank you for starving me, which forced my adaptation in macronutrient consumption to ultimately align it with the physique I was creating. Thank you for the long, intense workouts I endured to preserve my sanity. Just, overall, thank you.

Fasting, extreme treks, and isolation. This has been the way to finding yourself since the dawn of time. So now I found and created a "new age" way of doing this while in the SHU, which was self-inflicted adversity. I mean, in all reality, I could have just laid down all day and sought pleasure at every turn with drugs, with the brownie on the dinner tray, with the buying of snacks out of the store's canteen. But I fucking chose purpose. I chose purpose over fucking pleasure, which in turn gave me the most pleasure of all.

Fasting, extreme treks, and isolation. This has been
the way to finding yourself since the dawn of time.

And to any of you pussy-fucks who think instant gratification is what life is about, I have one question: Have you ever had a massive goal and attained it? It is much more pleasurable than that instant gratification—that brownie on your prison tray or the ability to sleep in a few extra hours. Trust me, it's much more fulfilling.

ARE YOU A FAKE-HARD?

When you change your thinking, it's the only way you can truly change your outcome—thus changing your life. In the pen, it's flooded with what I like to call fake-hards. As I've established, this is a bunch of dudes who look hard. They act hard, but they don't live hard. In my entire life, the biggest realization came when I sat in that mirror and I said, "Wes, you're a bitch. You're a fucking bitch. You fucking look pretty damn hard. You look pretty damn hard, but you're continually doing what puts you in tears like a soft-ass bitch. Period."

Every problem I ever had came from chasing money. That easy route. Dope dealing. Robbery. Those fucking easy forms of getting money, where I thought karma wouldn't catch right the fuck up to me, are where all my problems came from. Trust me, karma always catches up to you. And if a man is right, his world will be right. When I started to apply the wisdom of the ages I found in the books of men who overcame life's struggles, when I started applying these universal laws like karmic debt, my whole life changed. I started to see everything for what it was.

Every problem I ever had came from chasing money.

That dude with the tattoos on his face who's got straight titties and he can't stick to anything he truly wants? He's fucking weak. That tat on the face, that fucking rough exterior? Honestly, he just wants a hug. I was the person who just needed to fucking sack up, to create the validation from within with my actions. I was walking around fake-hard for so fucking long. It's crazy. Everything I did was the easiest way possible—and that's what people think winning is.

Winning is being strong enough to fucking lose. Winning is being strong enough to not let shit faze you. When a man fucking yells at you, you don't seek validation through that man by fucking blasting him in his motherfucking face. Strength is created through your daily process and the steps that create strength within, by choosing to become your best self daily, by choosing to act in a manner that you don't necessarily want to act in, to become your strongest self for those rough days. And you best believe that life will hand you all the roughest days to test your motherfucking ass.

Adversity truly introduces a man to himself. And I was around all them soft-ass bitches. Straight-up soft as fuck. I'm sure some of them watch my videos or even read this shit right here and they're like, "Fuck that dude Wes!" But then they go in the mirror and they realize it's the fucking truth. Hard truths fucking work.

So, of course, "the truth will set you free," but for me it's, "the harder the truth the better." You'll no longer have these hang-ups and these fucking insecurities that you've had your whole life. When you do one thing, get the fuck up and work for it. That shit is straight-bitch when I see a man who is obviously living with a set of fucking circumstances that are fully under his control to change and he chooses not to. It's a bitch.

*Everything I did was the easiest way possible—
and that's what people think winning is.*

It's a bitch being broke because you could get off your ass and fucking handle business. If you get rid of them vices and work fucking hard, I guaran-fucking-tee it. If you have that long view and you have that ten-year plan, you can be successful financially. You're holding yourself back. You're being a bitch. You're being fake-hard. You're working for a fake set of circumstances. You can be fucking ripped. You could have the best relationship if you quit fucking thinking about yourself and falling victim to selfish desires.

Some of the lamest shit I ever hear is grown-ass men who need to "go do this." Or they want to "go do that." Motherfucker, get yourself to a place where it's not even a debate to go drink with your buddies or take that whole pizza to the face and feel like shit later. Pleasure becomes a fucking form of weakness. You only link pleasure to re-fucking-gression. Straight-up regression.

And here some people are telling me, "Oh, Wes! Oh, oh, big Wes! You need balance." Balance, motherfucker? My overly fucking exaggerated extreme lifestyle is my fucking norm. It's only extreme to you, and balance is a term for low-level motherfuckers with a limiting belief system. Be rare. Be obsessed with your goals. Stay stubborn as fuck with your vision.

People complain that San Diego is expensive. Honestly, it's your problem—nobody else's. Plenty of people can pull it off. Why the fuck can't you? There are 51.9 million millionaires in the world (and it's only rising). Get your fucking shit together. Start solving some problems. Handle fucking business. When you aren't in your own way all day doing that fake-hard shit—collecting fake money the fucking easy way, with no real fucking dedication, no real consistency—you have no real pride for the attainment of the result. So, you fuck it off like I did. That fake-ass hard shit—always running to the fucking needle, always running to the bottle. Fake-ass hard, fake-ass shit. That is the opposite of what defines a man.

When I fucking realized I was a fake-ass motherfucker, I just stepped right into all the truth. And guess what? I wasn't fake enough NOT to share it with you motherfuckers. Speak the fuck up. Motherfuckers need to speak the fuck up because guess what speaking the fuck up does?

Guess what the fuck speaking the fuck up does? It holds you to it. It holds you to a certain lifestyle. It holds you to a certain set of principles. People don't speak up because then they have to live it. Now they're in trouble because if they don't live it everyone sees how fucking fake-hard they are.

You stacked that plate. Now it's your
fucking time to clean it up.

And I saw them all in the pen. "Wes, Wes! Big Wes, I'm going to work out with you, bro. I'm going to run this in. I got three years left. I'm coming out jacked." These motherfuckers end up quitting like bitches every time. Ding! They hit the bell because they ran up that dope debt. They had a conversation with their girl they couldn't take. Getting up early every day? No. They couldn't handle it. It was too much for them. Don't you fucking ever whine about how much food you need to eat when you were just claiming you were fucking hungry. You stacked that plate. Now it's your fucking time to clean it up.

But now I can't even fucking put into place how many motherfuckers make me proud lately. There is a shift taking place of enlightened individuals. They're up before me, probably on the East Coast most of them, but yeah, whatever. Still! They're checking me. They're holding me accountable—and I love it because I ain't letting them fail. I won't let them fucking fail because I'm a man of my word.

All your parents, or the fucking mentors of your bitch-ass youth, told you this: A man is nothing but his word. Why the fuck do you think you could break it on your diet or your training plans or your promise to take care of your fucking wife and kids like a motherfucking man? The biggest thing that keeps a motherfucker down is his fucking vices. I fucking personally know. My biggest hindrance was the alcohol and the drugs—the pleasure-seeking, the partying.

If you don't step up to the plate to fucking progress, you don't get it, and that's where the conscious-congruent living comes into fucking play.

When you're purpose-driven, everything's easy. Everything is easy with that ten-year plan. Motherfuckers want ten-year pay in two years. I was talking to a real estate agent buddy of mine from the pen one time. He told me he was making *X* amount of money, and it was clearly not what he was expecting. I said, "Motherfucker, you sound like you're down on how much you're making. You don't understand the correlation? You are two years in. You're getting two-year pay. Be objectively optimistic, motherfucker! Not biased to self, which will cause you to prematurely tap out."

In twenty years, you get twenty-year pay, if your heart's in it, if you don't bitch out and refuse to comprehend shit at the level needed. If you don't step up to the plate to fucking progress, you don't get it, and that's where the conscious-congruent living comes into fucking play. Every morning it'll tell you to do more. More is your fucking avenue for your progression. Progression is fucking life.

I don't give a fuck if you made $10 million last year. If you don't make $11 million this year, you'll feel like less of yourself. You're already used to the fucking $10 million. You need $11 million. And you need to push yourself to that next rep in your set with your exercise. You need to push yourself to that next day without cheating on your diet. You need to push your people and show them you love them by being the best version of your motherfucking self. Love is a verb.

ABIDING BY CONGRUENCE

While in the penitentiary, living this purpose-over-pleasure lifestyle, I found myself in complete alignment. I was walking in congruence with my conscience. My daily actions and habits were in line with the exact future that I was envisioning. When I was getting the fuck out of penitentiary, I knew that without fail I must stick to my daily process—my daily wake-up time, my morning reflection, my morning growth process, my training, and my nutrition. These were the things I knew would keep me in a state of inner peace. None of these actions caused me regret, ever.

In our lives, when we conduct ourselves in a manner that causes regret, we are immediately taken out of the moment and attached to a past event. To live in the moment, to operate at our highest vibration, highest frequency, we need to stay without regret in our lives. I needed to stick the fuck to my morning process without fail, or I would have regret.

And so, when I got out I knew my path, and my purpose was to teach what brought me inner peace. I had been suffering from mental anguish my whole life. I always had everything everyone talks about. I just always had trouble mentally. I always suffered from negative self-talk. I struggled with accepting life, and that's because I wasn't embracing the struggle that is life. I needed to sit with it, sit with the pain until I found a process that worked for me, which is this one I adopted in the penitentiary.

On the other side of those bars, by far the hardest pleasure to stomach every day was that early wake-up time. But it was so powerful forcing myself to commit to it, even when I didn't want to. I needed to chase my life's purpose. Breaking something as pleasurable as deep sleep to get up and create your best self is the epitome of fucking gratitude for any day you've been blessed with. So yeah, it was hard every morning, but that's why it was so effective. I would start my day with something that was difficult, and that continued to show me who the fuck I am. Adversity introduces a man to himself.

---

*I struggled with accepting life, and that's because
I wasn't embracing the struggle that is life.*

I want you to look in the fucking mirror. Are you pushing yourself? Do you have a clear glimpse of who you are internally? It's clear who you are during that early fucking wake-up: someone who crumbles in the face of adversity or someone who rises. And it's just the purest depiction of that to force myself up every morning at 2:45 AM for thirteen years straight in order to chase personal development, my best self, and create the individual that I admire most so that I can give him away.

Now, most people have trouble getting up early, and I do too. But the first thing I do is magnify my self-talk and make sure I'm grateful for the fact that I can get the fuck up; then I couple my slight negotiation with getting up so early with the love I have for my wife and my son and how proud I want them to be of me. So I'm infinitely powerful at that moment through these emotional motivators that rise me up well before the sun every fucking day, now and forever. It's not about me at that moment. It's not about how I feel. It's about my purpose.

Most people are going to fail at this because of how they feel. They don't want to get up. They don't fucking *feel* like getting up. So they just lay it back down. In all reality, they just showed themselves that they're pretty selfish. They want to do something, but they don't really feel like it. The universe was calling them to become more, but they really still believe their path is their choice, not answering the call of their conscience that would lead them down the path to their ultimate purpose. So they lay it the fuck back down and miss that first step, which was to illuminate their path to true purpose.

5

A RARE MOTHERFUCKER

(Acquire What You Admire)

We know what we admire in others, so we must acquire that.

The rules that garner respect for us as individuals are non-negotiable.

Stop fucking chasing shit. Draw it in. These universal laws are what must truly govern us. If you want solid people around you, be solid. If you want respect, conduct yourself with respect. If you want love, love your motherfucking self. I'm a deep individual. I'm committed. I'm loyal. I'm loving. So guess what? When I didn't have that for years upon years while incarcerated, I decided to give it to myself. And when you act in this manner, you draw in the correct people.

All too often I see people chasing people. FUCK chasing! Make yourself so fucking *rare* that people come to you because you are the top choice. The truth is you set yourself apart by conscious endeavor—action. You did what they're after. And you did it with proper intention. Attaching proper intention to your vision is the game changer.

Simply put, acquire what you admire and let your core values govern. Don't ask nobody. It's exactly what you want for yourself. So be it. The way you see yourself, your character, your look, however you want to be—be that. Go get the job you fucking want. Get that tattoo you want. Work out to create the body that you want. And it's not in a selfish manner. That's what's most important. The intention is selfless.

I created everything that I am today because these are the things I admired. I admired those dudes in the pen who had the fucking utmost respect toward all individuals. They took their time to speak to a motherfucker and share what worked for them in life. You could feel that they wanted the best for another individual, but they weren't bitches about it. They were like, "Nah, motherfucker, this is how it's done." That's what I like: individuals who speak and live the hard truths most avoid. Hypothetical is hypocritical, so to speak some wisdom and fail to apply it across the board is just a massive lack of awareness.

Attaching proper intention to your
vision is the game changer.

So, really, just wake up! Just shut the fuck up for a minute and look in the fucking mirror. Your conscience will tell you which way to take this day. Is there fucking shit you got to change? Yes. Is it okay to be happily dissatisfied while being proud of yourself and wanting to work harder? Yes. This is a great place to be.

Is it okay to be disgusted with yourself? Hell, yes! I remember when I would wake the fuck up, hung over as shit on a bender, and just be like, "Fuck man, things have to change," while in tears. Meanwhile, the night before I was running with pure shame glorification, trying to glorify the mentality of, "Damn, I was way fucked up last night." And really in my heart I knew I was wasting my life; I was wasting my potential.

Today, anyone who crosses my path, I can't even leave their vicinity without just being like, "What's your passion? What are your goals? What are your dreams? What are you going to do?" As soon as I know, I can encourage them forward, just as I want to encourage you. Don't get further away from where you want to be. Don't do that shit. I want everyone fucking expanding always in all ways. So when you're done with my programs, this book, or watching my content, I know I've heightened one's level of awareness to a multitude of mindset tactics to unlock their greatest potential.

Is it okay to be disgusted with yourself? Hell, yes!

THE OTHER ROUTE

Before the penitentiary, I was falling victim to societal standards of what success appears to be. I was after money, that's it. I needed more fucking stuff and didn't care how I got it. I was after the fast life and relaxing while massively capitalizing at any cost was what I admired. We've been fed this image since the beginning that one day we *win* and then just kick our feet up on the beach and don't do anything but live that lavish life. We finally retire.

I was living the endless pleasure-seeking lifestyle, chasing what I thought I admired from everything society and entertainment implanted into my head. When I found that fast money, I bought a brand-new Range Rover on 24-inch Asanti rims, white on white. I had the nicest condo in downtown San Diego. Meanwhile, I was still chasing other things I admired, which meant easy women, alcohol, partying, "good times," and drug use—all the bullshit that is completely not aligned with someone who has moral standards.

When I finally sat down for a moment, I realized that chasing all of the above, identifying with it, and admiring the wrong things got me exactly where I didn't want to be. I admired the gangster life. No, fuck that. I glorified the gangster life. I watched gangster movies. I grew up on *Scarface*, *Goodfellas*, the works, and it just looked like who I wanted to be. I realized too late that these movies end in a manner that nobody wants: to fucking live in the penitentiary. While I was incarcerated my eyes were finally opened. I was starting to see the flaws in that whole lifestyle most people glorify during youth. I really started to see the truth about those characters and that life.

I really went within, got truthful with myself, and I realized that the work was the gift. I felt great after it. Instead of trying to validate myself externally with everything that everyone else thought was cool—and anything I thought made me feel good—I focused on being true to myself and doing what actually made me feel good through and through. I started limiting my food intake, working out much harder, and above all, being a better person. I would go out of my way to help the inmates who couldn't see this route. They were still chasing the drugs. They were still chasing the easy money. They were still thinking that the fast life would make them feel whole. And they were continually causing themselves unspeakable pain from this pursuit.

So, I just went the complete other route, which was directly in line with what I say life's purpose is: the creation of the individual you admire in every way so that you can just give that person away. Every day has been a relentless pursuit of creating this man I admire—his physical appearance, actions, demeanor, and energy—so I could give him to those around me. In doing so, I was bringing my fellow inmates up and truly experiencing a state of self-love and contentment I never knew before.

In the penitentiary I ran across Whiskey, who was from the San Gabriel Valley. Whiskey was in his late thirties, a white boy covered in prison ink who grew up in foster care. He was actually foster brothers with the rapper The Game. Trust, me I actually direct messaged The Game and asked him, "Is this your foster brother?" because it seemed too far-fetched, but it was not.

Now, Whiskey was in there for drug use this time, but he had been in the penitentiary before for murder, drug sales, and drug use. He had been in the penitentiary his whole life after leaving that foster home where he had seven brothers and sisters. He and other inmates like him were just grown-ass kids. They're older than me, but they're grown kids who never truly matured. So I took him under my wing. I would not let him use dope anymore, and I showed him how to live a disciplined lifestyle.

I pushed my penitentiary program on Whiskey and the others to build them up, and it worked, as it does every time. At first, they hated me. They hated me because I was so strict. I pushed the rules and the prison politics upon them to where they had a mandatory workout, mandatory wake-up time, and then—since they told me they wanted to progress in their physique—I put mandatory restrictions on their diets to help them. I showed them how to track their macros in prison using books that had all institutional serving-sizes. Nothing was perfect, but it was better than the spreads others were making. I was on their case.

During this time I was already on Instagram. I was starting to push the positive quotes, thoughts, and topics that were going through my mind. Most of this I would retrieve during my morning reflection period when I would sit in the stream of consciousness and just absorb all the wisdom that would carry me through each day. I was sharing online and I would always share with the fellas around me in my workout car (the group of guys you work out with in prison). I would just see their eyes light up. It empowered them just like it did me. The quotes and belief systems I shared—and still hold dear to my heart—changed me and I knew they would change them.

I remember telling them stories about when I got busted. I remember the way they looked at me because there was a time when I would look that way at Big Block from IE. Big Block was in his early forties with a huge belly, just a straight-wreck motherfucker who was always carrying a massive 10-inch knife, ready to stab anyone when it kicked it off. He was such a liability that he gave me fucking anxiety. I even remember telling Whiskey and my workout car about Big Block, how crazy he was, and seeing the way everyone was reacting. I knew I had become to them now what Block was to me back then.

I gave them anxiety and made them feel uncomfortable because of my intensity, but I knew I was doing it from a spot of inspiration instead of from a spot of manipulation like Big Block. He was very violent and very ruthless. This is how it is in the penitentiary. People don't get it. It's a dictatorship. You follow the fucking rules or you're going to pay the price, and the cost is massive. Most of the time, it's your life.

Nevertheless, I kept them accountable to who they wanted to be. We shared deep passages with each other from books we were reading, and we built each other up from within with these affirmations and these *core* beliefs that we held deep in our hearts. But, yes, we were in prison. And, yes, we still had to follow the politics that were above us.

Like all motherfuckers who suffer from low self-image,
they started losing discipline when I was gone.

I basically had the keys to the building the second I came in because I dropped points from higher-up yards. I say basically because Pup, a satanic skin from Lancaster, still had the block until he left after a few months, but I was already leading the guys from day one. I was in control of everybody of my race in the building, but there was somebody higher up who had the prison. And then there was somebody higher up who had all of California. And so we all had to listen to somebody higher up than us.

My point is that I was in control of these guys, and I was going to show them the best route to bring them to where they needed to be. They hated me at the time, but as soon as I was gone you better believe they were messaging me, wishing we were back where we were before. Like all motherfuckers who suffer from low self-image, they started losing discipline when I was gone. They started getting back into the drugs. They started experiencing the pain that comes along with not being the person they admired, and not walking in alignment with the person they were trying to create—the person they respected.

Once you fully solidify your core beliefs, you finally say, "Never, never again."

Over time, day in, day out, I would just teach these dudes, building and strengthening them through repetition with these affirmations and these activities. We were building character and confidence through action, and I was helping them return to the free world as assets, as opposed to the liabilities they'd been their entire lives.

Whiskey got out, and he started fucking up again. He would always message me when he was fucked up because he felt that guilt. He felt that regret I've previously explained: karmic debt. And the worst part is he always believed in what we built. He knew the truth, but he kept falling victim to that dope life.

Once you fully solidify your core beliefs, you finally say, "Never, never again." That's how we start building the vision that creates the life we want for ourselves. We cannot deviate from a plan that we know worked for us mind, body, and soul just because it's difficult. The truth is that because it's difficult is why it works for us.

RESPECT

Respect is earned. Respect is earned. Respect is earned. In the penitentiary, all you have is respect and your word—and out here it's a lost art. The rules that garner respect for us as individuals are non-fucking-negotiable. What do you respect? Do that. What do you admire? Be that. Acquiring what we admire is the task of a man, and it's the life of a man. In the penitentiary, and in that criminal life, we did it the wrong way. The real way is doing what's really hard for you, which is being stern with self and kind to others. I've been on yards with a lot of guys who had everything just twisted. But I understand them because I had it twisted until I looked deep within and said, "I'm fucking up. I'm fucking up. I can't be this way."

When you're sitting in isolation and solitude, this becomes real fucking obvious. When you're causing yourself this much pain, you're obviously the problem. You're being dealt that pain because you're giving that pain. It's an unavoidable universal law that we get what the fuck we give. When you stop giving pain and you live in a proper manner, you will get the outcome you want. If a man is right, his world will be right, and these fail-safes, these gems, these quotes, this wisdom have been everything to me. This shaped who I am. When I'm working out, when I'm training, when I'm dieting, and when I'm dealing with vices or tough life situations, I'm just saying these over and over in my head.

Through repetition, we strengthen ourselves. We strengthen ourselves past anything we could do through any type of outward stimulation, with consistent inward reflection. It's got to be internal. Any external stimulation will fail you. And at that, we're losing it, you guys. We're losing our touch with our spiritual selves and we aren't powering up our spirits. We're losing it because we're attaching to the material world too much. We need to spend time with ourselves every day. A man is more useful when he travels alone because he reflects more. He's more useful when he travels alone because a motherfucking man reflects more.

It's an unavoidable universal law that
we get what the fuck we give.

We need to reflect more on who we want to become. When we make the subconscious conscious, we can become all of it. With a proper plan, we will become financially secure, we will get ripped, and we will have the demeanor that every superior man should have.

And even the shit I fail on, *again*, regret is your guideline. When you fuck up and you regret something, that's the universe giving you a hookup. You've now received a signal as to how you can fucking change for the better in order to get where you need to go.

Anything you regret, it needs to go. It doesn't serve you anymore. If something doesn't serve you, it must go. That goes for foods, drugs, or any type of vice. I refer to anger as a vice because I seek pleasure from it, from the anger, from the negative reactions of people. I get pleasure from it. That's why I do it, and the point is we can't fucking do this. We will always be punished through lack of presence for our negative energy exchanges, even when no direct action is taken.

We need to be purposeful, and we need to realize that when we're seeking pleasure, we're either harming ourselves or someone else. We can get pleasure in many other ways, but it should be purposeful acts coupled with delayed gratification that gain us pleasure. You can take more pleasure in your sacrifice and your commitment to your goals than you ever could just getting handed them outright—without the work, without the journey, there is no worth in making yourself fucking less confident, less secure.

In the penitentiary, fools just spend all their money on snacks, dope, and all this shit. And then they don't realize that over the years they got themselves somewhere and turned themselves into someone that they can't even face in the mirror. So, pleasure comes in so many different forms. We need to limit it.

When we work really hard, when we sacrifice everything we want in order to be the man we were supposed to be— to create that character and conduct we admire—then the most simple pleasure suffices. Sitting on the couch after a hard day's work can mean more to you than buying a fucking Bentley if you work hard enough. If you didn't work for that Bentley, it won't fucking mean shit to you—it'll be here today, gone tomorrow. When I sit too long in my Rolls seat it hurts my fucking ass just the same. When we exceed the bounds of moderation the greatest pleasures cease to please.

Without the work, without the journey, there is no worth in making yourself fucking less confident, less secure.

To be spiritually unfulfilled and have everything materialistically can be the most detrimental life possible. I've been elevating myself financially, acquiring material things lately, and it's detaching me from my spiritual self. I don't want to lose it, so I'm going to level up. I'll test myself. I'll push myself harder. I'll fucking make sure I keep that spiritual attachment.

Are you making sure you have that spiritual attachment? Does all the small shit mean a lot to you? Are you losing it? Everything small should mean the most to you. If not, you're not thinking deep enough. You're not preparing your mind to absorb these times. All we have is the moment. All we have is a moment and that doesn't mean go live and enjoy that pizza and drink that drink. That's not living in the moment. That's trading today's happiness for tomorrow's.

Living in the moment means creating a program and a life that satisfies you in every way. It means putting your heart and your soul into your acts, spending free time with your loved ones, pumping them up, and bringing them up with you. A true friend can make you do what he can. That's what I'm here to do. I'm here to show you guys. I was in that pain. I was in the SHU. I was in that shithole. Those dudes don't make it out because they didn't figure this out.

Living in the moment means creating a program and a life that satisfies you in every way.

Some people are locked in their own fucking prisons out here, and I know how to unlock it. It's the hard work. It's the pride in self. You could have way less and love it way more. You could also have everything and have the right perspective and love that just as much. It doesn't mean because you have shit you can't respect it. You just need to prepare your mind for it. You need to go through exercises like this.

FROM ADMIRING TO ADMIRED

When I grew up, my dad was a plasterer. He worked every day as long as I can remember. Since I was born, on the daily, he left at 5:00 AM and came back at 5:00 PM covered in cement.

I always admired that he was so much harder than me, harder than fucking everyone. And so, in the penitentiary, when I really sat down and realized what I admired in individuals, this came up. I just knew I needed to be that hardworking man who got up early and gave it his all every day. Now, since getting out, I knew my level of discipline was being admired by people around me. Even as I got out, my mom started to be more disciplined with her diet and exercise.

I started to rub off in a positive way on everybody around me. Everyone I knew who was trying to get me to go out and party, drink, or whatever the fuck, I would sit down and talk to them. I would talk them out of it. I would literally tell them where those actions would land them. And they saw what happened to me.

I chased pleasure so much that I landed in the penitentiary. Most of my friends have been very close to going, or they have gone to jail or prison before. I just came out sticking to my guns and not breaking. There was no flexibility on what meant the most to me: my personal development program. Honestly, 99 percent of the time, your friends aren't helping you further the evolution of your consciousness. I needed to make fucking sure I was being a true friend, which was keeping them out of harm's way—even if that put me in it.

I've become the man who I've always admired—the man who lives for his family's happiness. And it really is the most fulfilling thing ever that I can wake up every morning and say, "Fuck what I want! As long as they're happy, I'm good." And to me, that's what a man does. A man is a protector, a provider, and above all, a man, by definition, is responsible.

Honestly, 99 percent of the time, your friends aren't helping you further the evolution of your consciousness.

As always, I continue getting my inspiration from the wisdom of the ages, books filled with quotes from everybody from Confucius to Albert Einstein. Lately, what's really resonated with me are the beliefs and teachings of Marcus Aurelius and all the stoic philosophers. Since the beginning, they've always been the hardest—living the hardest, needing the least, and being extremely accountable to themselves.

They always operated with the highest level of accountability within themselves. The stoic system and stoic philosophies are void of a victim mindset. What resonates with me most is that we're fully in control, and that's what motivates me in the morning as I read my stoic teachings. When I finish reading, then I go about my day in that manner.

We all have to understand that mindset is everything. I've seen people who have everything, and they're so fucking miserable because they don't stack their small fucking wins. When you get your wins, you can't be stopped. No one can tell you you're a loser. You create pride from within. You earned that PMA (positive mental attitude), and that is everything. Why am I so fucking passionate about this shit? Because I got energy. Why do I have energy? Because positivity charges you. Negativity drains you.

When you see someone with this much energy, who doesn't stop and takes no days off, it's because they're positive. When you see someone who can't stick to their shit, it's because they're negative. And the best thing about that spectrum is that you can change it tomorrow.

All these moments are passing so fucking quick.

Are you negative today? Get the fuck up. Change that shit tomorrow. Don't fucking go drink and get yourself in trouble.

91

Don't shoot that dope. Don't sniff that line. Don't end up in the pen. Don't hit that person. Don't do it. Love your fucking kids. Love your friends. Love your family. You can't make everyone see how you do. But my job out here, my fucking purpose in life, is to let everyone see what they really got. And what you really got is a blessed life that you should be grateful for.

I've seen so many people lose their lives. So many people lose their lives in prison. So many people lose their lives to the system. You don't know what you got until you lose it, you guys. Take this time, sit down, and write everything you're grateful for and never fucking forget it. Get that shit tattooed on your fucking chest. Rub that shit in your chest. Rub that shit in your fucking chest and just fucking realize the truth about all of these moments. All these moments are passing so fucking quick.

The most foolish thing is anybody who says, "Oh, time passes so fast. Time flies." Well, guess what? If you have the proper program, the proper discipline, the proper etiquette, the proper life and work ethic, then you can fly to your goals and not fly into that bag of shit you've created. Let's fucking get it.

6

NO REHEARSAL

(Habitual Construction & the Program)

Like most people who grew up in modern society, I lived a life based on perpetual pleasure-chasing. Simply put, my selfish desire to seek pleasure created an extremely weak mindset. It altered my subconscious into being easily negatively influenceable. I only sought pleasure and linked pleasure with what life was meant to be; any time something got difficult for me as an individual, I would no longer see it through—I tapped the fuck out. I discovered personally how people's habitual pleasure-chasing created a mindset that wrecks their long view and any chance of achieving their goals.

Waking up late. Eating fast food whenever I wanted. Working out whenever it was convenient for me during times when I had motivation. Drinking every night. Smoking weed throughout every single day. Everything I was doing was for my own pleasure and benefit, and that perpetual pleasure-seeking led to a sense of not even being attached to life. I couldn't enjoy the grandest of things because I simply would just overdo it.

I would overcompensate with these acts of *relaxation* and this fake fucking made-up vision of what living the great life is— which most people still have. Most people live in that manner and they don't realize that true sacrifice and pushing themselves daily to increase growth mentally, physically, and spiritually are the keys to cultivating inner peace and contentment.

---

*I couldn't enjoy the grandest of things
because I simply would just overdo it.*

Seeking easy money. Seeking consumption of shit in bags and bottles alike. I became disgusted with myself because I let my physical appearance falter, which led to a significant decrease in confidence. I was so weak that I would seek the easiest route in everything I did. Where the fuck did that get me? In the goddamn penitentiary. There I was, feeling like a loser because of the choices I made. And my choices landed me in the worst place possible.

DO YOU TAP OR NOT?

Your habits, self-investment, and daily process are the most important aspects of your life. Your level of success will never exceed your level of personal development. Success is something you attract by the person you become.

That voice in your head that's screaming at you, getting louder and louder, for you to make these changes—that's your conscience, motherfucker. As I've established, that's your higher self telling you to step up and showing you how to be in alignment with your best self in order to live your best life. The only path in this life is what your higher self is supplying you. It's not a fucking *what if*. There is no what if. This is who you're supposed to be. You don't feel right because you're not listening. Why aren't you fucking listening?

Stop thinking you want the result. It's not the result you're after. You're after the person you're creating through the process. This person cannot be stopped. You're creating someone who won't fucking tap when it gets tough. I don't give a fuck what you want. When it gets impossible, do you tap or fucking not?

Your level of success will never exceed
your level of personal development.

If you seek to just look a certain way and not live a certain way, you're entirely focused on acquiring—you're not about becoming; you are fake as fuck. The real ones seek to become strong by taking the hardest path. The hardest path gives you the most fucking pride in your conduct. And pride in your conduct holds you to your goals.

So, what the hell does this come down to? It's obviously long view and heart. If you have heart for ten fucking years, you will be the top of your shit. And better yet, how about twenty? The twenty-year plan never fails. I don't give a fuck. Most people spend twenty years trying so much different shit that they never get their result. If you pick something and you stick to it with all your heart, you'll be the top of your game.

Ultimately, can you sit the fuck down, be quiet, and spend some time getting to know your fucking self? To know your answers? When you get to know your answers so clearly, there's no fucking way you can tap. And what are the answers? It's a *who,* not a *what,* motherfucker. It's the person you're creating, the one doing the work. That's all you can see, coupled with a vision so fucking intense the work involved is irrelevant, the sacrifice is irrelevant.

I was sitting in the BMU(behavior management unit) on the way to the SHU with a life sentence on my head, and I still stuck to my vision. You think a little fucking baby coronavirus lockdown will deter a motherfucker who's had his life on the line? My life was on the fucking line and I still stuck to my vision. I still dieted. I still trained. I still read. I still found my answers. I still chose *personal development and self-mastery,* as we all should. This is who you need to be. This is what I'm talking about. The success is a byproduct of who you create during hard times. It's a byproduct of the motherfucker who won't tap.

If you pick something and you stick to it with all your heart, you'll be the top of your game.

I can sense *your* energy, the way you carry yourself, and your demeanor from a mile away. From this, I know exactly how much you put in today, and everyone else does too. I can tell from a mile away if you put a hundred in today or if you fucking hit that bell and bitched up. Getting your wins daily in alignment with the *vision* you have of you at your greatest potential is a prerequisite to living out your life's purpose.

The most sickening thing about the streets is everybody can just choose to live a lie and show what they want. In the pen, it's all on blast. You're on blast. I know what you're doing. I saw what time you woke up. I saw how much heart you had in your workout, and we know exactly who you are. There is no hiding.

The fact is the rules that garner respect for us as individuals are non-negotiable. The thing about challenging yourself and having pride in your conduct is that your self-talk changes automatically. You can't fake this shit. Everybody's trying to read about it and fake it instead of pushing themselves, becoming proud, and watching that self-talk follow suit.

The real ones only see what remains to be done. We only see what remains to be done. I look at wherever I'm weak. I zero in on it. *Fuck that. It can't happen.* When I was around all these motherfuckers and I walked straight into the most savage fucking chow halls, on the most violent prison yards, I felt weak. I felt like I wasn't fucking confident enough, and they could sense it. Hell, I could sense it. It was fucking obvious. It repulsed me, so I had to find the answer to overcome this feeling that was paralyzing, and it came through my daily personal development process.

You motherfuckers need to extinguish weakness. And you extinguish weakness with fucking action. You can't tell yourself you're someone you're not. You need to get up and earn that shit.

In the penitentiary, it's built around proper programming. It's a militant program based on your dedication, discipline, and how you conduct yourself as a man. There is no weakness. We will ensure you expel your weakness. You're showing up to every workout. You're waking up at a mandatory time each day. There's non-negotiable acts all day long that you need to adhere to for the greater vision of your group (gang) as a whole.

Inside, the pleasure-seeking can only be sought through the drugs. And at that time of my life, I could see that shit for what it was: a crutch. That shit was such weakness, and it always ended badly for the users. These guys would get fronted drugs because they didn't have the money. And then they would routinely get stabbed for not paying up, or they'd just get fucking high and cause problems with their own race or other races by not paying their debts or being late, resulting in disciplinary action.

I was no longer using anything to seek the pleasure or *relaxation* I thought was doing me good on the streets. At this point, I could sit back sober and realize the work I was putting in was truly causing me to love myself, build myself, and keep me from falling backward headfirst into those vices.

That was self-love that I was creating within. I was habitually constructing this high level of self-worth. I was increasing my capacity for love. And my actions were in alignment with who I wanted to be. Through my habits, I was creating the person I admire. I was finally, for the first time, in love with the person I had become.

NO RESULTS
(PRIDE IN YOUR STEPS)

In Chapter 5, I mentioned my boy Pup. When we met, I walked in knowing that everybody in his block could feel my commitment. They could feel my fucking energy! I was seven years into my ten-year prison sentence. In truth, before I arrived Pup from Lancaster had the block. That means he had the building. He had the keys. He was the one in control of all the white guys. I walked in knowing they would see and feel a motherfucker who operates at a completely different level than they'd ever seen. I still had three years to go and I was fully committed to running the tightest program without a single break in schedule. Because at this point that was my character, and it was what I validated myself from.

Habitually, I had constructed a man internally who validated himself from his daily conduct overall. He was more in tune with the steps that would gain him the result he wanted than the actual result itself. At this point, the steps I took and the intensity I brought each day meant more to me. And the man who can take more pride in the steps it takes to obtain the result than the result itself can never be stopped. I couldn't be stopped and I knew it.

So, Pup had the block. I walked in and I helped him. I saw that he was on meth and I knew that I could get him off this because I could see it in his face that he didn't want to live this life. He was going through it. The drugs were no longer causing him any pleasure; it was just pure pain written all over his face, massive regret. He would stay up all night in this self-inflicted agony from meth, like so many do in the penitentiary. I took him under my wing and I said, "You're working out with me." I built him into one of the strongest guys in that building. Took 30 pounds of fat off him and got him ripped. He reached a point where he would do many fucking muscle-ups on the pull-up bar, lifting himself above it. We ended up calling that dude "Muscle Pup" as a joke.

Many years later after we all hit the street, anyone I came across, even Pup, would say, "Man, I wish you were still around because you kept me in line. It's a lot harder now." They were falling victim to their vices again. But at the time, I was able to instill progress within them.

The man who can take more pride in the
steps it takes to obtain the result than the
result itself can never be stopped.

I inspired Pup to be his best by fucking living hard as fuck while showing how amazing one feels when aligned with a greater purpose, which is the main thing that I always preach. As I'll explain in Chapter 8, you create the man you admire in every way so that you can give that man away. And that's exactly what I did by personifying my teachings and coming in with such energy that Pup wanted to listen. I had the physical results. I spoke the talk and walked it like a motherfucker.

When I was back on the streets, I took everything I learned in the prison system and I made it very simple. I would stick to my wake-up time of 2:45 AM regardless of how I felt. I would always go into my reading of positive quotes and books that really resonated with me directly after I had my coffee. After that, I go into an intense workout, journal, and then make videos—which are solidifying these positive affirmations in my head.

With my morning process, I have rewired my mindset, totally reconstructing my subconscious to become someone who will not deviate from his personal development program. Today, my program is everything to me because I believe we do not ever rise to our goals—for we shall fucking fall to the strength of our system. And my system has brought me from ten years in the penitentiary to being a multi-millionaire CEO of my own corporation within two and a half years of my release.

As my company grows, I need to implement massively complex variables and complete challenges involving people and technology. Every day, I need to overcome these tasks that cause most to just fucking tap out. The man I created over the years incarcerated will not quit for fucking anything. The man who never misses that wake-up bears the same mindset I need to push through the difficulty of business tasks that pile up. I created an optimal individual who will always see it through regardless of how tough it gets. And I accomplished this through a simple process of wake-up time, reflection and intro-spection, meditation, my proper diet and training, and carrying that positive mental attitude (PMA) throughout my day with me.

We do not ever rise to our goals—for we shall fucking fall to the strength of our system.

I bring my PMA to business, ensuring that any success therein is a byproduct of my personal development. The man I created in the penitentiary now runs a company, and I share him with people in the masses, helping them raise their level of discipline, self-respect, self-love, and everything in the process.

If my old self needed to fulfill my current position, it would not be possible. And I consistently come across people in my coaching program who quit because their stress management level is too low. I give them a very simple task, one they fully understand they can pull off, but the fact is that they quit too easily before seeing it through. A lot of people out here are failing to connect the dots. And my old self would have been the same person tapping out, seeking another joint out of frustration, and *relaxing* through a long week. Fuck, with 2020 I know my old self would be right where I left him and worse. He'd tell himself he just needs that one drink for a bad day. That would turn into ten drinks and he'd be set back three to four days.

The fact is, today I'm the one working while others are out partying. They're sleeping, and I'm already training in the early hours of morning. This is what set me apart when I hit the streets again. The fact that I would and will never give or take an excuse when it comes to accomplishing my goals and dreams is what made me elevate myself so quickly. From my program and what I teach, I know that if you believe in discipline as the precursor for success, and in your ability to develop the person and habitually construct this mindset—that you cannot be stopped—you will be able to elevate yourself as quickly as I have.

THE PROGRAM

In the penitentiary, I was the individual who literally would not break program for anything because in that setting it is one's only source of validation. People would look at you and say, "Damn. Motherfucker does not miss a day of that workout ..." and they would see in your physique that you've slowly done your time—time didn't do you. You learn from this because when you see everyone else, you see they're not who or where they should fucking be.

Ultimately, this is deductive reasoning. As you see what not to do and who not to be, you reach a point where you're focused on what you *should not* do, rather than what you *should*. Too often, people want to add fucking more to their life instead of taking anything away. And it's actually much easier to just take away the things we regret and cause us so much pain and replace them with positive actions, which is so much more natural.

I will forever stress the importance of our daily process. Our morning ritual is habitual construction. As I share my morning routine with others, I'm actually showing them what they receive from a hard workout: PMA. That shit is unavoidable when you push yourself to your highest potential in physical activity.

As you see what not to do and who not to be, you reach a point where you're focused on what you should not do, rather than what you should.

First, we gain that PMA through the workout. Then we go into reflection during and after the workout. You need to understand that during a workout, a run, or anything of this nature, you're in a biased state. You are in such a positive frame of mine, endorphins flowing so rapidly, that you see everything perfectly.

You have all the answers. Even your worst situations are now positive. You need to understand this is all perception. When you go back to a really harsh time when everything seems impossible, you know it's only your perception shaping that moment and making such events seem so drastic. It's all in your mind. The same event can be looked at from two massively different sides of the spectrum, simply by perspective.

I like to say nothing in life truly changes, but our perception does. I've been in arguably the worst places on Earth and I kept a better outlook than I had in some of the best places on Earth. That's why I know the effects of a PMA exist. That's why I know it's nothing more than our frame of mind. Our morning process ensures we solidify the correct mindset and get our aim for the day. Once we shape that frame of mind, we have a much better outlook on everything we'll face that day.

So, the *during* of a workout is fucking key. Let's focus on our self-talk. Even in the midst of a great workout, some people are not fully engaged, and they're in a negative state. They're stuck in the mindset of, "Fuck this! I hate this shit. This is bullshit! This isn't what I want to do." When it comes to anything that's good for us, we should never have negative self-talk about it. At this moment, our self-talk must be savage, affirming, strengthening, and it sure as fuck needs to be approving of the actions we're committing to in order to further our lives.

Our morning process ensures we solidify the correct mindset and get our aim for the day.

Talking ourselves out of something that extends our life (like exercise, healthy diets, behavioral and habitual construction) is foolish. This is what people do every day. Really successful people often realize that the only thing holding them back their whole lives was their negative mindset.

When we gain a positive attitude toward strengthening our weak points, strengthening ourselves, we can make such drastic changes and progress toward our goals faster than we could ever imagine. The reflection process is truly powerful because you step into it and you grab gems (quotes and frames of mind) that further your progression with increased clarity, negating energy leaks. For me, I remember one such gem being, "Life happens for you, Wes." Anytime I come across something that I'm not particularly enjoying, I gather this powerful understanding during my morning ritual and carry it with me all day.

People don't realize you can turn even the most negative situation or event into a positive one. And I learned it during my ten-year sentence. The whole fucking time I was thinking, *This is turning me into a beast. This is making me so strong. Nobody can stop me. I'll never break. I'll never bend, never fold. I'm never losing.* Ten years of positive self-talk. Now, I can't break. I'm unstoppable simply from my self-talk.

I will never quit on something I truly want in my heart, ever. It will never happen because of this self-talk, this affirming belief system that champions cultivate. They cultivate that by knowing failure will fucking propel them forward—not by being afraid of it. It's when we hit rock bottom that we really meet and get to understand ourselves.

Adversity introduces a man to his motherfucking self. The real world forces us to fucking draw in a lot of the material world, and it's a good thing because we need to live. Still, it takes us away from the spiritual world. The morning, when everybody's asleep, when you haven't gotten into bills, problems, or the material aspects of life, is a great time to jump into the spiritual aspect. Otherwise, it's too late. The material aspect will always detach you from the spiritual world.

You need to separate these two times. It doesn't need to be in the morning. Honestly, that's the best for me because I haven't yet been bombarded with life. I haven't really been on my phone that much just yet. I haven't had any true problems jump into my face. I'm able to tap the fuck in much greater and see everything I'm grateful for in my life. And, as I'll share in Chapter 7, gratitude opens the door to everything.

Adversity introduces a man to his motherfucking self.

Overall, strengthen your process and make the subconscious conscious. Doing so means we're no longer a victim to our mental states. Our past is where our subconscious fucks us. My subconscious tells me, *Wes, you have a massive anger problem. You have rage. You have all this shit built up from the time you did and all the things you went through in your life.* Okay. Then I can always tell myself in the morning that I need to be kinder. *It's stronger to be kind.* I can focus on everything I need to get me where I want to go and keep my ass out of prison. I can focus on my objective, which will help me toward my goals.

We achieve goals faster, we recreate ourselves, and all of us are habitually constructing ourselves into the persons we want to be. We're learning to step back in our minds and say, "This isn't me. This is my subconscious. My past is causing me to be a way I don't need to be anymore because it doesn't serve me. This no longer serves me. This isn't me." When we learn to unmake this through our process, we become so much more aware. We're woke, motherfucker. We're woke as fuck. We see this shit happening, and we understand our self-talk.

In closing, let me tell you about two convicts in the prison kitchen. One dude, he's washing the dishes like, *Motherfucker! I hate this shit. Eight cents a fucking hour!* The other convict just learned to wash the dishes and he's like, *Holy fuck, watch how fucking good I wash these fucking dishes. Watch how good I do this shit. Watch how calm I am. I feel so fucking strong.* Who do you think ends up in a worse position? The bitch with massively negative self-talk or the man positively validating himself through his task and self-talk?

It's as simple as that. Shit. All I see out there is grown-man-size hissy fits. Have I done them since I've been out here? Fuck yeah, I have. Did I call myself a bitch after? Fuck yeah, I did. Extreme accountability's the answer. This is 100 percent the fucking answer: Waking up, reflecting, exercising, reaching that PMA, and checking our self-talk.

If it's good for you, or if it's your responsibility, never tell yourself you hate it. You are strong as fuck, motherfucker. Tell yourself. You think the best of us reached their best lives thinking, *Nobody suffers in sacrifice like me for my end goal ...*? Get the fuck out. You need to do some shit right now. Who gives a shit? You're the best at this. Earn your best life. Become more aware of your mind and pursue full control. You're the fucking best at this. Get your motherfucking outcome. You have one life. This is *not* a rehearsal.

7

GROWTH IS LIFE

(Facing Tests of Gratitude)

Before I got busted, I don't even remember ever using the word *gratitude*. I truly believed that someone could not be happy unless they were consuming a substance. If I saw someone who was enjoying themselves and having fun, I thought they must be drunk or high, or they just made a bunch of money. I never believed it was an internal feeling we can cultivate at will. So, as I've explained, I was always just chasing those external forms of happiness, and this was due to the idea that pleasure came in the form of acquiring things.

Gratitude is motherfucking action.

For my ten years in the penitentiary, I was removed from everything in life. I was no longer able to seek happiness through a bag or a bottle, or through monetary gain. So I learned to look within. Most importantly, I learned that gratitude is a feeling we get when we see what we have as enough. This shifted my perspective forever because seeing what I had in prison as enough enabled me to stay grateful. Now, on the street, what I have is enough, and I remain in a grateful mindset.

Today, my happiness is derived from what I have, and that means my conduct, character, and my discipline, which then turn into a lot of financial success by helping others. My daily process strengthens and builds me. It gives me confidence, self-respect, and self-love. And transferring these things to others also brings me the utmost fulfillment.

Gratitude is motherfucking action. It shapes the landscape of your mind, and being grateful positively impacts your perspective. Your perspective is everything. You can have the same motherfucking problem and look at it two different ways, depending on whether you're in a positive or negative mindset. One of the biggest problems I see out here is people failing to understand how to get themselves in a positive mindset. From my experience, I find that they are usually stuck in a negative mindset while engaging in deep, complex thought. A word of advice: never do that. Never seek to decipher your life's problems while in a negative fucking mindset. Doing so creates a safety zone for habitual negativity.

I'm inherently negative. But I understand how to create habitual positivity through my daily acts. If you're inherently negative and you're having problems with negativity, you need to create positive tasks and habits on the other side of that—and make them non-negotiable.

Every motherfucking thing is earned. We must earn positivity by doing the uncomfortable shit that negates that negativity. Nobody is fucking negative after a hard workout, so that makes for one quick way. Nobody is massively negative after deep introspection, so that makes for another way. Nobody is fucking negative after a day of helping people and doing stuff for others. You need to create a day based around positive habits—the harder for you, the better.

When you're facing a problem, reshape your mindset by going straight into positive action, and then return to the problem. When you're in a negative mindset, everybody fucking knows that sometimes something as small as getting a speeding ticket can just fucking send you off the motherfucking deep end. Later, once your mindset changes, you're like, "Oh, well. No big deal. I ain't even tripping ...." That's the power of the mind. And that aspect of your mind can be yours to control if you understand how to shape your mindset through positive acts.

In Chapter 7, I shared a little about my program. Self-reflection is obviously important, but it's specifically great to get the day started with some gratitude. I will never be able to stress enough how critical it is for us to wake up early, grab something positive to read, and start making those affirmations to move us toward that grateful state. Adding this shit to your routine is life changing.

Outside of the books, and within yourself, one of the easiest ways to separate yourself from a negative mindset is to be deliberate about your thoughts when you wake up. Try opening your eyes and focusing on the thought, "How can I serve everyone best today?" Anything other than that, you're trying too hard to capitalize and you're forgetting what we're all here to do. Also, it's the gateway to a victim mindset. When we're trying to gain too much or trying to capitalize too hard, we're forgetting what we're all meant to do here, which is to heal our *pain* and teach others to do the same.

PROVIDING TO OTHERS

While in the penitentiary, I taught different mindset-strengthening tactics and used affirmations and positive influence to help people. One of the things that I would always tell them is that we strengthen ourselves by needing less and doing more.

So the individuals who can actually find a lot of pleasure in not being pleased—in no longer needing external forms of validation—they will be a lot more grateful.

My crew—Ryan Wagner, Pup, Whiskey, and Frog—and some other inmates would sit in my group and I would tell them all these thoughts I was having. Specifically, I would encourage them to see that we don't need much. In all reality, overconsumption of food is the quickest way to not be grateful for food. Following that line of logic, we looked at this relationship in reverse.

The individuals who can actually find a lot of pleasure in not being pleased, they will be a lot more grateful.

Through hunger and fasting, we realized the value of nutrition. Through sickness, we realized the value of health. Through fatigue, we realized the value of sleep. And a big piece of having beneficial realizations was through taking away our most simple of pleasures and our most simple of necessities. Later, we could bring that shit back and we could be grateful when we exceed the bounds of moderation. The greatest pleasure is to please.

Often, inmates perpetually pleasure-chase in the penitentiary. So they'll just eat foods that taste good and wash themselves up. They'll just keep doing heroin and speed, drinking alcohol, and doing these drugs to feel good. Eventually, their substances lose effect and they find themselves addicted and chasing the high. My point is that when you're pursuing change, you need to restrict yourself on the immediate pleasures of life, which will in turn raise your baseline discipline level, helping you fight your true vices and triggers with strength and clarity.

A big piece of having beneficial realizations was through taking away our most simple of pleasures and our most simple of necessities.

When I'm sitting on my rack, training hard, I'm restricting food by dieting, and I'm giving myself less sleep. By providing less comfort to myself, I avoid going out of my boundaries. The second I give myself all these pleasures (eating too much, sleeping in too long, or working out less), all of a sudden I'll find myself driving out of boundaries. These tactics of limiting basic needs kept me from traveling outside the fence mentally and victimizing by overthinking what I had lost.

Humans are the only animal whose desires increase as they are fed. Whenever I gave myself these small pleasures, I would realize that it caused me to desire more and more of the things I no longer wanted to chase. It took some time for me to learn that our power doesn't come from our accumulation of riches—it comes from moderating desire. You're truly not ready to be rich until you no longer desire riches and you're not ready to be off lockdown until you no longer need to escape your circumstances.

Here people say, "But Wes, you have a Rolls-Royce and Lamborghini and all this stuff ...." Yes, I do, motherfucker! It's purpose over pleasure—*not* no pleasure at all!

The people who actually stay grateful and produce results at their highest level are the ones who know to moderate desire. As they accumulate success, they know the importance of self-inflicted adversity in mastering success and actually keeping it. Ultimately, comfort is the killer of dreams, even in the penitentiary. I taught my crew to live harder—as if it wasn't hard enough doing five to fifteen years.

Whiskey was in for four years for dope sales. Pup was doing five for dope sales. Wagner was doing eight for attempted murder. And Frog was doing fourteen years for attempted murder. If it wasn't hard enough during all this time, we restricted ourselves even more in order to gain more strength and be more grateful. And fucking let me tell you, on the days when we gave ourselves a little something extra, we really enjoyed it.

THE SHU

Segregated Housing Units (SHU) are the most militant places on planet fucking Earth. Cold-ass, dark-ass fucking cells. Every day, you're going to wake up to roll call at 3:30 AM. My longest term in the SHU was fourteen months. First, I would hear the Southsiders call out each of their homies by name and say "Dias." I remember the Southsider shot caller, Casper. He had the most savage voice—deep, crazy, and demonic. Now, I will say this shit was just a life-changing experience because I didn't see what he looked like for eight months. When I finally saw him, I was shocked because was fucking white. Then I thought about it, and the friendly ghost was a good fit. The homies make their names fit the way they look. They're always good at that shit.

After the homie Southside roll call is when the white boys do theirs. We call out to our people. We say, "Good morning." We give the notification that we're up and we're program-ming—because you need to be up programming even if that cell fucking door ain't opening. Next, you go take your showers by 4:00 AM (unless your tier is rotated to nights). After showers, you have breakfast, and then you start getting ready for yard.

Every fucking time in the SHU, when you go out to yard you're bringing something you shouldn't be bringing. You're hooping something, *gangstering* your shit, as some of us would say. Basically, when they're checking your body for anything you shouldn't have, you strip down and you show the guards your butthole. But there's an opportunity when you're getting back in line, and you basically pick up whatever you shouldn't have after you're stripped out. We would usually bring a braided rope out with us to do pull ups in the corner of the cage.

Let me fucking tell you about some militant shit. We would be doing shitloads of burpees out on the yard. Straight militant, we would call hard and soft counts. When I was doing my burpees, I was going "One, two, three." Then my cellies got the hard count, "One." Then I count three again. Then he'd say, "Two." And this would go until we reached twenty-three on the hard count.

This is how it is in prison. Understand the California prison system. Understand who people are when they're in there. I always tell it like it is. When you're in prison, you get down with your people. You're not fucking going against it. You're dealing with some fucking cats who don't give a shit about what would break your little heart. The SHU's meant to break you, and it doesn't break them. This shit will break you. They get used to it. They adjust.

There was a time when my celly and the other white boys were fishing some dope. Fishing is when you have a shoelace from cell to cell. You throw anything heavy, and you slide it from under your door all the way across the building under the other cat's door. If you don't make it, he slides out and gets you and he pulls you in. You attach some contraband and you pull it back. They had some black heroin in an envelope and they were fishing it cell to cell.

Now, they were pulling a 50-paper (50 dollars' worth) of some heroin in a rig. When one of the white boys pulled it too quick the wind caught the envelope and smacked it against the wall. And then a cop fucking grabbed that shit. When he came to the window, the white boy was clearly *gowd* out (meaning he was high on heroin), and he's like, "Hey, man … oooh." He's all, "Hey, give me my mail. I need my mail."

Then the motherfucking cop looks in the paper. "Oh, you need your mail?" He knew it was a rig and some dope. "Yeah, whatever the fuck."

Now, keep in mind the SHU showers have locks on them. The guards took us all out of our cells and they threw us in there. And they made us fucking sit there for three fucking days in these wet-ass, gross-ass showers. They did this because they were trying to get somebody to snitch. A real youngster, James, was their main target because they thought he would crack. Fuck that. We just kept him strong. We're like, "Hey, fool. You're going to be good. This ain't shit. We're all here together. Don't trip. We got you. Just fucking ride through this and I got you when we get out."

He got used to it. He adjusted. We all got the fuck used to it. We fucking adjusted.

Now, the SHU is just always grimy. If the SHU ain't already bad enough, try being there on a fucking hunger strike. Holy shit, all too often people ask me, "How do fools in prison stay in shape?" Easy answer: We work out all the time, and we don't eat shit. As I was sharing with regard to self-restrictions, if you want to get somewhere in life, just start taking shit away. That's how you build true discipline, which is the prerequisite to success in all areas of life. If you want to get to know yourself, take shit the fuck away. If you want to get somewhere physically, take shit away. There's nothing you're going to fucking add to your life that's going to make you stronger.

I happened to be in the SHU on the last fucking big-ass hunger strike. We couldn't eat, but luckily I was stacked up at the time. The cops weren't even tripping. Usually, they put all your shit in brown paper bags. This time, the cops weren't tripping. Everything was good. They were allowing us some more canteen than we usually should have in our cells. So we were eating. Still, they weren't too crazy about the hunger strike. They filmed us all, and they gave us all charges for being part of it. We each got 1/15 for being part of it.

But, just like the odds of someone snitching, there are always fools who try to go against a strike. They'll be like, "Oh no, dude. Fuck that." They're already getting weak as fuck about it. Like, "What happens if I eat?" I told one fake-hard, "Motherfucker, you better not, man. We're telling you, you're not. You're not eating. I'll shoot you a soup and some beans every day and that's all you get. You'll be fine."

I mean, those are the fucking times that really make you enjoy life. If you want to really get to know yourself and enjoy your life, like I said, take shit the fuck away. Check mark the wisdom of Fyodor motherfucking Dostoyevsky: "Suffering is the sole origin of consciousness." Watch how good that fucking plain-ass bologna sandwich tastes after you've been on a hunger strike for ten days. Depriving yourself will do things to you mentally that you'll keep for you the rest of your life. Like, fuck, them pancakes are going to be pretty fucking good when you get them.

Never-the-fucking-less, the SHU is the most militant place on Earth. It's the most savage. You'll be living structure 24/7. They'll make sure you're up at 3:30 AM. They'll make sure you're going to work out every day—even when the yard doesn't open on weekends or whenever the guards want to fuck with you. Hell, sometimes you don't even want to fucking go out cause it's a buck 10 or a buck 20 in them cages. You're like, "Fuck that shit. I hope they don't run it." But no matter the case, even if they don't run yard, you're still working out.

If they do run yard, you're going out with your homeboys. We would run ten sets of 88 burpees. Meaning, I'm doing 88 and you're doing 88 until we collectively hit 880 burpees.

And you might be asking, "Wes, why 88?" Well, it's not my fucking choice, but I'll tell you. 88 = HH = Heil Hitler. Again, I'm not racist. Racism is the epitome of ignorance, but in the pen you won't change these fucking things. You won't!

While I'm posting my shit online, I always catch grief in the comments. I hate it. I can tell they think they're being so badass: "I don't even know how it could be like that. Why don't you change it, Wes? Why doesn't it change?" Seriously, shut the fuck up, dude. It won't change, okay? Live with this shit. And honestly, don't go to the pen. If you ain't tough enough, then you need to turn your life around—because guess what? You ain't tough enough.

I wasn't tough enough. I needed to force myself to be tough enough. It was ten years of tears, of pain, and of missing everyone who I didn't see one fucking time. You ain't tough enough. Straighten your motherfucking life out.

TEST OF GRATITUDE

We all call it the hero's journey when we go through pain and return with wisdom from our experience. One of the biggest mistakes a lot of people make is thinking that everything we learned, or our wisdom, is commonplace. I was like that. Now that I'm out and sharing what I learned, I find myself receiving so much positive feedback.

There is not enough fucking time on Earth to make all these mistakes yourself, so you better learn to learn from the fucking mistakes of others.

I meet all kinds of people who can put themselves in my shoes and see life in a new way. Most of them basically say, "Wes, I don't even know what it would be like to not see my family for ten years. I don't even know how you're strong enough to sit in a cell without leaving for fourteen months. This makes me just so grateful for everything I have today." To pass on our experiences so others can steer clear of that negative path is everything. There is not enough fucking time on Earth to make all these mistakes yourself, so you better learn to learn from the fucking mistakes of others.

Just like that, through my story, they experience an automatic, massive perspective shift on the fact that they could lose everything today. Why does everybody think we have so much time? We need to prepare ourselves every day because life is coming, whether we like it or not.

We must strengthen ourselves by being grateful and using every moment to our advantage. We need to do this so we can create the individual we admire with the intention to just give that individual to the world. We share the hero's journey—everything we've learned, all our pain, all the wisdom we've gained—in order to help each other along the way.

Years after hitting the streets again, more recent than fucking not, I had a profound moment. I was driving to the gym and I had tears streaming down my face. Tears of gratitude. In the depth of my soul—from what I've been able to overcome and the feeling I have inside, how proud I am of myself, of my friends, and the people I reach—I was overwhelmed with gratitude. And I carry that feeling with me every day.

I've come to the conclusion that life is very simple. And the answer to what life is all about is that it's a gratitude test. You've simply been blessed with a chance to live during this amazing time in any manner you choose. The only thing you need to do in order to enjoy it is remain grateful. And when you reach the point that you fully believe in your heart that life is truly a test of gratitude, you become invincible. Everything is a win, good or bad.

---

*When you live merely in the external
world, you exist only in this age.*

With this mindset, nothing can faze us. We simply know everything that happens is meant to strengthen us. It's meant for our progression. It's meant for the evolution of our character.

So, what is the opposite? What is it when we're not fucking grateful? It's selfishness. It's a lack of compassion. It's a lack of understanding. People tell me their life is hard; they don't want to live. I've had motherfuckers tell me they don't respect themselves. I hear their tone and I can see their expression and I can tell they have no compassion for themselves. Like, "Your life is hard compared to what? Compared to who?" I look around and nobody I see has it that fucking good. I don't know who they're comparing themselves to.

So there's an adjustment that needs to take place. It's very simple. We need to step out of the external world more often because *people* are becoming victims of external circumstances. When you live merely in the external world, you exist only in this age. This age alone is where you exist. When you step into solitude, when you embrace it and submerge yourself into it, you exist in all ages and all answers are provided to you in that moment through infinite intelligence.

In closing, fucking spend some time with yourself today. And then do that every day. Find your answers. They won't be the same as mine, but they'll be along the same lines. We're all connected. Much love and respect to you as you seek growth. And remember, growth is life.

8

GORY FUCKING DETAILS

(Your Story & Personifying the Teaching)

Through my time in the pen—fucking calling shots, having the spots (meaning yards and blocks in prison), and fucking leading people to be their best so that they weren't wrecks—I dealt with the worst, most hardheaded motherfuckers. The only way I could get through to them was by being a true leader, by truly embodying what I was teaching. When we personify the teaching others will wish to learn. When we actually get results others will wish to earn. The fact is that the truth will always get through to them. And, as we always say, the truth fucking hurts. So hard truths are a must!

When you deliver the truth, trust me, you'll deal with a shit-ton of pain. You'll be scrutinized more than anything. But guess what! A motherfucker like me can take that shit. I like it. I can't tell nothing but the truth. Now, I won't sit here saying I'm so real because I did time. Like, look at all my tattoos. Like, look at me, I'm buff. Like, this is why I'm real. Nah, fuck all that shit. I'm real because I'm going against who I was my whole life. I'm real because I have no problem telling you the real fucking way it works, telling you the real fucking way to live your best life.

Because I pursued a path of validation through external means, I put my efforts into securing money and power.

You can choose right now. You can fucking look within and say, "You know what? This stupid-ass shit I'm doing ain't serving me. It ain't getting me where I want to go, and I don't feel good about it. And it is a choice I'm making." You can choose to follow the motherfucking blueprint I share with people on the daily. You can choose the hard way. The real way.

The guys I grew up around with nice cars, they were already self-sufficient. In a weird way, they didn't have any choice in the matter. They just had places and they had money. Their foundation was success; they didn't receive that the hard way and they sure as fuck didn't get it the real way. They weren't good teachers to me because they didn't tell me what to do or how to do anything differently. They just instilled a desire to have what they glorified, which was financial success at any cost.

If they had been great teachers, they would have told me, "Hey, you shouldn't live in this manner." But they put their shit on a pedestal and I worshiped it. I was so oblivious I was drawn to it. And because I pursued a path of validation through external means, I put my efforts into securing money and power. Ironically, that's fairly aligned with what society tells us a man should have.

So, let's get this straight. I've always personified the teaching. But before penitentiary, I was teaching people how to be more gangster, how to be negative. I learned from my favorite movies, *Scarface* and *Goodfellas*. I valued the negative traits of people and I was building them up in my mind into figures I admired. Honestly, I think most of society admires them. There's no debate that America has glorified the convict and gangster lifestyles throughout cinema, media, and beyond. I found out the hard way that neither of those lifestyles are anything to be glorified. I also discovered that a quality teacher should always seek to cure people of the actions that will lead to the pain that we ourselves experienced.

Before the pen, I was moving large amounts of marijuana and engaging in criminal activities that landed me in the penitentiary. So there I was, personifying the teaching in a negative way. Fuck, I was great at being a horrible example for the people around me. They would follow me, so I got a lot of people in trouble, including myself, by bringing them along.

Negative leadership is a massive hindrance in today's society. When we know we're doing something that causes us pain and we promote it to our people—instigating them to come along with us into something that could be detrimental to the evolution of their character—this is the shadiest act we can choose. This could be as simple as knowing we have a problem with drinking and inviting others with the same problem to a night of bingeing. This can be even more foolish as we are not only committing a criminal act, but pumping up people around us to ride with us. This is the dumbest shit known to man. And we will pay massive karmic debt for our decision to directly involve others in the pursuit of pain and suffering.

---

*Fuck, I was great at being a horrible
example for these people around me.*

So, I pumped my people up on pushing weight to live a baller lifestyle. We would get large amounts of marijuana, make large amounts of money, and spend large amounts at the club—drinking bottles of Cristal, bottles of Dom P, doing coke and speed, being pieces of shit to those around us, elevating ourselves with these fucking monetary possessions, and thinking we were better than people. Essentially, it just created a false sense of validation. That false sense soon turned into a massive downward spiral. Nobody ever wins from this lifestyle.

THE POWER OF YOUR STORY

When it comes to spending years in penitentiary, getting out alive takes you stepping up. It takes you being a leader. It takes you personally guiding people around you to become assets rather than the liabilities they've been their whole lives. Most of them have been or currently are addicted to drugs. Some of them are doing time for violence. In all cases, they're in the pen for falling victim to their negative habitual traits. To bring them out of it you must become the leader. You need to steer them away from the most common problem that humans participate in.

We consistently try to convince our minds of something our heart knows is a lie. In order for a true leader to step up, they need to denounce everything happening externally, look into a person's heart and know (a) what they want and (b) what will align that individual with their desired outcome. Overall, they need to see what will bring that person to their highest poten-tial. Leaders will only see this in others when they have healed themselves. That is to say, we can only heal others once we've healed our-fucking-selves. In that healing, there is now a story worth sharing.

When people tell me, "Wes, you're a good storyteller," I say, "It's hard to fuck up your story." I think most people fuck it up by censoring reality. Share your story verbatim. Don't leave out the details—these help people connect to you. If we connect, then we can lead. The most personal shit to you is more likely to affect the people around you the most. Don't just share, "Oh, I made (X amount of money). I felt great. Look at my abs." You can't just share the good side. If you don't share the details, the challenges and failures, then you won't be able to help anyone get through it. What's most personal is most general.

We consistently try to convince our minds
of something our heart knows is a lie.

In the penitentiary, I was dealing with the fucking biggest of liabilities. People choking themselves out in order to shove a needle into a forehead vein. People squeezing their junk to shove a needle into a dick vein. People shooting up in any vein possible just to get high—just to numb themselves and not be present during those years when they could have experienced exponential growth.

You need to be present for your pain, and I'll say that a thousand times or more. Presence during the painful times is when growth occurs. Nobody grows during all these fucking pleasure-seeking activities. When you're getting your way, you're not growing. Change when it's uncomfortable. Get the fuck used to it. You need to stand in front of the mirror and realize that your comfort is fucking killing you. When you're growing and you're learning lessons, you need to apply those principles to your entire life.

Most people, they'll listen to motivational and life coach quotes and they'll apply them to one area of their life. It's not exactly inefficient, unless you're the comfortable motherfucker who's only looking to elevate the area you're strongest in. Look at your fucking weak points to really level the fuck up.

Dudes in the pen, they would be on dope, they would still have to get their program done because of the racial politics, they would do some crazy fucking workouts. I saw an old celly of mine in the SHU do a shot of black (heroin) and do 120 pushups in one fucking set. Now, was that fucking amazing? Obviously, yes. But his weakness was still fucking him over daily because he wasn't consistent. It was only when he was high as fuck that he was able to push himself and not let his mind hold him back. When he didn't have dope he was too sick to perform.

When you build pride in self and you build confidence from overcoming hard, difficult tasks for yourself, you will always win.

You need to improve your weaknesses, not simply focus on your strengths. He was using his weakness to feel strong. Overall, you should only initiate the timer toward achievement when your body starts giving up. When you feel physical failure, that's when the mind kicks in. I've seen motherfuckers get five years over a hypodermic needle in the pen—five years over their vice and that fucking needle in their fucking body. That timer just kept resetting for them.

Turning a liability into a true asset will be the most beneficial part of your business, your life, and getting yourself through tough times. Turn your fucking liability of self into an asset through intense self-reflection and self-commitment. When you're committed to something that's difficult for you, what do you fucking build? You build pride in self. When you build pride in self and you build confidence from overcoming hard, difficult tasks for yourself, you will always win; you have a different energy when you consistently overcome the adversity put in front of you.

I don't fucking worry about speaking anymore. I don't care if I need to speak in front of 500 people, because I speak all the time and I hammer it. I want you to be that way about your workouts. I want you to be that way about your diet. I want you to be that way about business. I want you to be that way across the board in life, realizing that all these small steps—the ones that everybody overlooks all day—are what creates this. Confidence is simply the byproduct of consistent implementation.

In the pen, I met this kid called Books. His story always hits me in the heart, to this day, from the amount of commitment someone can make overnight. He was a really smart twenty-five-year-old from Hemet, California, who got slammed for bank robbery. He was doing nine years. Just before we met, he quit being a bitch and he stopped doing drugs cold turkey. He came up to me and said, "I'm working out with you tomorrow." I told my boy Pup, "Hey, Books is going to work out with us tomorrow. Let him do what he can, and when he's done with what he can, we'll put extra on him. He'll do what he can, and then we're going to heart-check him, see where he's at."

We must take pride in strengthening our weaknesses and becoming an asset across the board.

The next day, we let him do the same workout, but with a few less reps. At the end, we were heart-checking with some burpees. When he was fully done, I could see in his eyes that he was feeling it. Then we put some more on him. Not only did he stay there the whole time, this fucker was present during the pain. His self-talk was strong and affirming the whole way through the workout. I could feel he was truly aligned with the internal outcome we wanted for him. He was present during the process and he pushed himself. And guess what? He walked away proud.

Fast-forward about three years and he still hadn't missed a day. He would go to school, come back, and do burpees with me. He would go to yard with me and hit the bars. I took someone who was a liability in the physical department, and I turned him into an asset. This is what we must do in our lives. We must take pride in strengthening our weaknesses and becoming an asset across the board.

Responsibility educates. A leader, by definition, is responsible. As a leader, you know your motherfucking route. So step the fuck up. Be the one who steps up. Take pride in being able to call yourself a failure when the people around you are not working at their optimal level. In all reality, your weaknesses are what invite their excuses.

I needed to create these assets around me, because in the pen that's the only way I would fucking get home. In business, that's the only way you'll get your outcome. How do we fucking create the assets we desperately need to excel out of the liabilities? We personify the teaching.

They need to fucking see that it's working for you in all ways. I won't fucking listen to you unless you actually embody what I wish for myself. So make sure before you speak—before you try to push it on other people—that you're ready. Make sure that you're there personally. If you're not, it'll have an adverse effect.

When you teach others to get their validation from self, when you teach them to get their validation through character, you can change anybody. Why do I know? Because this is how I changed.

ALIGNMENT

I believe in alignment. I believe in complete alignment to one's vision. It's difficult to create the person you want to see in the mirror—your highest self. It takes work. It takes sacrifice. The only reason people aren't reaching their ultimate goal—constructing their vision at its highest potential—is because they're not willing to invest in themselves. They're too lazy when it comes to the work. They think there's an easier route.

In basic terms, my journey involved seeing traits in individuals who had a certain level of physical appearance or personality and mindset that I admired, then putting all those aspects together to create my optimal self. I created the person I admired in all ways with true wisdom, work ethic, and knowledge. Be it parents or teachers, many of the people who are pushing their beliefs on others are not fulfilling the package because of selfishness. Caving in to their selfish desires is what's keeping them from becoming everything they need to be, physically and mentally, in order to be the correct teacher.

I have an online community with over 2,000 members and I remember one of them asking, "Wes, how can I get my son to listen to me?" I told him, "He's not going to listen to you. I wouldn't listen to you. You don't even fucking listen to you." And that was the biggest thing that he needed to hear. He doesn't even listen to himself. He doesn't even listen to the vision he has for himself and the promises he makes to himself. So, how and why the fuck does he expect his son to listen to what he's fucking saying?

If we personify the teaching, then others will wish to learn from us. I've become such a great teacher out here because I've selflessly given away so many pleasures and made so many sacrifices to create that teacher I personally needed to see. People tell me all the time, "I identify with your message because of who you are and because of who you've created." That is what I know to be true because I will not take advice from someone who's not in control of themselves.

How can a man step up, who's obviously out of control, riddled with vices, overweight, and falling victim to so many negative aspects of life?

We must embody the teachings in all areas. Therefore, the wisdom we share must be unbiased. If we say something like, "The way we do anything is the way we do everything," we are not just standing on our strengths and looking at them as a trophy of who we are. We are magnifying weaknesses and ensuring the wisdom we speak—the quote and credo we live by—is applied across the board to our weaknesses, as well as to our strengths.

For my clients, and for my team and group members, I teach that they are the path. Their construction of self is the path. I tell them our life's purpose is to create the individual we admire in every way so that we can give that individual away. We are all essentially pursuing the creation of what we truly admire. The daily work and sacrifice is insignificant because the vision is so strong. When creation of this vision is paramount, we can actually help our people instead of being someone who's just suggesting shit while living in a hypocritical manner. Don't be a fucking fake-hard, full-of-hot-air motherfucker with a lack of adherence to whatever you're teaching.

All pursuits start off extremely juvenile and elementary.

At first glance, with me, people might think they're just getting physical training because I do have an imposing aesthetic look. Once they go deeper into my program, they all realize the exterior we are creating is simply a byproduct of these deeper principles that govern us. It's the deeper principles that I teach. The individuals in my program learn those deeper principles and they apply them to every area of life.

So we're not just teaching someone to build a physique. We're looking at the intention for which it's created. The purpose of our pursuit is so much greater than the actual pursuit itself. When that purpose is selfless—when we wish to help, when we wish to cure people of their pain by first curing ourselves—we will have a much greater outcome than from the selfishness of pursuing an external change.

All pursuits (internal, external, financial, etc.) start off extremely juvenile and elementary. In the penitentiary, the physique was no different. I was approached because some of the homeboys just wanted to be physically imposing, to have the presence of someone who's strong, who can take care of themselves. I was approached because they wanted to be ready for straight war because that's what prison is—there are riots and stabbings all the time and we needed to be ready. But over the course of the program, they realized there was a whole greater agenda, which was to create the character of someone who had a mindset that was non-negotiable.

So, at first, the endeavor begins as something elementary. When you earned your first paycheck as a young person, you didn't say, "I'm going to take this check to the bank and create generational wealth." Hell fucking no. You wanted to buy yourself something. You bought a CD or a video game. And that's okay. The pursuit starts off elementary and we grow with the process, which gives longevity to the growth process of the simple phases of life.

When we're young, love starts off as just the most superficial form of pleasure. We want to touch the other person, to kiss, embrace, and have sex. We just want that feeling. We're not loving in the mature sense because in a juvenile state it's just purely physical. Then, once we grow and mature, it turns into something deep and internal. It becomes a real relationship, real love and connection. This is not exclusive to coupling.

In closing, I don't want you to avoid or be afraid of having superficial motives at the beginning. Everything evolves in pursuit, even your purpose. What I do want is for your goals to become non-negotiable. As you create the person you admire, I want you to experience yourself growing beyond superficiality and discovering the deeper principles at play. Discovering those deeper principles is important because those govern everything about your life.

As you are creating the person you admire, I want you to remember that the real goal is to give that person away. Work through your story, share it in all the fucking gory details you experienced, and personify the teaching. Get it and give it the fuck away, because the true measure of a man is how others leave his presence.

9

NO DAYS OFF

*(An Ultimate Lifestyle Through
Conduct and Character)*

I'm completely over the fucking belief that everyone's out to get you. It crosses my path all too often lately, and it disgusts me—so many victims out here. For yourself and all those you love, seriously, stop that bullshit where you think everybody's shady. Do you fucking understand that when you truly believe this, you're actually drawing people of that character into your life? Honestly, in my opinion people who think everyone else has ulterior motives are the fucking most shady individuals out there.

The way we view the world is a confession of character. And guess what! If you want loyal, loving, hardworking, trustworthy people around you, you need to be that in the fucking depth of your heart. You can't just approach life thinking people are untrustworthy right off the bat, while simultaneously drawing in quality people. The fuck's the matter with this shit? It's the most fear-based, victim, bitch-ass shit—and I see it among fucking a shitload of men, scared as fuck to trust someone. "Oh, I've been hurt before." Fuck you! Be the change then, brother.

One of the realest things I've learned is that imaginary evils are fucking incurable. Meanwhile, on the daily, motherfuckers make up and worry about shit that will never fucking happen. Like, "Hey, let me completely ruin this relationship before it happens because I have trust issues." What the fuck? Fake-hard motherfuckers with trust issues, masking their fear with toughness. Bitch-made, bitch shit.

I'm hypersensitive to people's energy. The second people hit me with that shit, I'm calling them on it. I understand them, but I'm not gonna side with 'em. What I will do is enlighten them. I got snitched on by my partners and I did ten years. They fucking wanted to give me a life sentence. They told the fucking judge, "Don't let him out. He'll kill me." That was my experience, and I still trust people. I love people. I feel the good in them because I was way worse than the cupcakes out here. I don't even care about those fools who dimed me out. I don't give a fuck what they're doing. I'm onto new shit. I trust everybody. I don't give a fuck. I'm loyal and trustworthy to a fault, and I'd rather live like that than be a scared-ass bitch.

You can't just approach life thinking people are untrustworthy right off the bat, while simultaneously drawing in quality people.

Every single one of these truths that I share was fucking realized in the motherfucking mirror. Pure honesty at heart is what gave me these answers. When we're trying to convince our minds of something our heart knows is a lie, this is how we cause ourselves the biggest problems in life. Look within. You know the answers. Problems with trusting people are bitch-made. If you can't trust people, you're being a bitch; you're halting any sort of real relationship that could ever formulate. Trust. Give love. Don't be so fucking scared.

PERSONIFY YOUR POSITIVITY

I met Zach Lopez for the first time in the chow hall on the day I was moved from the high custody block to medium custody. White Boy, my old cellmate, pointed him out to me, saying, "Hey, that's your new celly over there. His name's Zach. He's a one-percent biker from the Moloch motorcycle club. And he's a good dude. I know him." And so Zach raised his hand from across the chow hall. He knew me. We mutually knew each other as acquaintances on the yard and through other people. When I let him know I would be over later that day, his first words to me were, "I'm clean, bro. And I keep it clean." He said this because bikers are known to be extremely dirty in their cells. I said, "Whatever." I wasn't tripping.

Once I was officially transferred I went to my new cell. Zach did indeed have a tight fucking ship. Everything was clean. Cleanliness in the cell is a massive sign of who you are in the penitentiary, how you conduct yourself, and how you just treat your surroundings.

I sat down and we started conversing. Zach's a great guy. The first things I saw were pictures of his twin boy and girl who were about five years old. His wife was pregnant when he got busted. He was inside when they were born, but he was able to see them during a visit. And the coolest things about his twins were their names: Bonnie and Clyde. Fuck, that brought tears to my eyes as I wrote it. They were his source of strength, along with his wife, Crystal, who wrote to him during his entire sentence. Zach's family was his emotional motivation to stay off drugs, to work out every day, and to be the best man he could be—given the circumstances.

Zach and I got to know each other pretty fucking well because we worked out every day. Not only was Zach a solid celly and a great individual, he actually held the keys to the building when I rolled in. The day eventually arrived when he was transferred to another block and he left those keys to me. Our trust was big. He wasn't someone who brought negativity to me unless it was a big event that would affect us both. He was never a bitch who pushed negativity on the next man, like so many who fail to be accountable to their internal state. That was an admirable quality to me in penitentiary and it's one of the most important qualities to me on the streets today.

In the penitentiary, you find inner peace; everything else, your whole external world, is taken from you. You find yourself because *within* is the only place that remains for you to travel. Zach had been down longer than me when we met. He found contentment and inner peace to the point where he didn't have to push his pain and his negativity on the next man, which I highly respect. Many of us fail at this in life. I feel very intensely the energy we put off onto each other—our universal language is energy exchange. The greatest thing we can do is be accountable to our energy at the root of who we are, and always share the inviting, positive vibes.

Zach was an accountable man. He understood what he was doing at all times in energy, thought, and action. He was a man who personified conduct and character; however, like many of us, he had his own struggles. None-the-fucking-less, he was a family man and he couldn't wait to get back to them. He could not wait. When he was finally back on the streets, he got his wife pregnant again. With a third child on the way, he returned to messing around with that old one-percenter lifestyle. One night, when he was leaving the club, he pulled out in front of an oncoming vehicle. He was struck and killed. This was within about two months of finishing his eight-year stretch.

If you cannot align with your higher self, your regret and your inner turmoil can most fucking definitely lead to something like suicide

---

I believe universal truths are unavoidable. They're all connected. If you recall the story I shared in Chapter 2, I was fortunate to say "Rest in peace" to the prosecutor who took her own life. I believe this was karmic debt. It was cosmic justice for how that individual was being paid. She carried such regret, such inner turmoil from her conduct.

I know people who have overcome murders and all sorts of heinous acts due to the fact that they were able to escape that life. After making changes and seeking congruency with their conscience, they no longer fell victim to their karmic debt. If you cannot align with your higher self, your regret and your inner turmoil can most fucking definitely lead to something like suicide. For Zach, the end result was similar. He couldn't give up the biker life. He lost the inner peace found in the pen. And the karmic debt that came with that one-percenter lifestyle caused him to lose his own life.

Each of us receives calls from our conscience. Until we learn to answer those notifications as the first step of many toward living our life's purpose, we will forever be lost. Otherwise, those calls become yet another set of tallies amassing in our karmic debt.

A MATTER OF CONDUCT

You might still be wondering how all of this originated for me. How did I start to speak like this? How did I become the motivator I truly am today? It was out of necessity. It was out of survival. In the California prison system, I needed to strengthen everybody from within, to build self-worth, so we could all get out alive. One liability in the pen could mean death, so I went through and reinforced my cellies and all the people around me.

I accomplished my goals through the program. The fact that I would be awake before many of my boys meant they would be up. The fact that I would work out longer meant they would too. When trying to help others make positive changes, our weakness is their way out, so we must become devoid of visible weakness. My boy Whiskey used to kill those workouts with me. Every day after chow we would do ten sets of thirty burpees, or thirty sets of ten burpees. Whiskey never missed a day on them bars when we hit that yard. He never missed a day of the burpees. That's just how we got down. But once I was gone he fell off, just like so many others who suffer from a lack of self-belief.

A successful man will continue doing plenty of things each day that lead to the evolution of his character.

For my celly Zach Lopez, the straight homie, the outside world competed with the program. His girl, Crystal, was a soldier and before the pen she rode with him—and he fucking loved it. Inside, she made him feel so loved. He was sober, he kept his shit straight, and he worked out tough. I had all the respect for him in the world. He never ever slipped on his program.

Zach was a great example of dudes you run across in the pen who were doing their time right—and you could fucking tell. But things change on the outside. A million times over, I would tell him, "Man, get out and do good." Once he was on the streets his lifestyle changed and his life ended on the road outside of a one-percenter club in San Luis Obispo. His conduct countered the program.

The program is how we strengthen ourselves. It's the daily shit we could easily pass up but we know we should do. Knowing the definition of success requires that you understand the common denominator. A successful man will continue doing plenty of things each day that lead to the evolution of his character. He does plenty of things each day that he doesn't want to do, in order to have the future he desires. This is counter to obsessing over pleasure-filled acts—all of that hustling, drinking, partying, and drug use. The second you think that pleasure will lead you anywhere you want to be, you're greatly mistaken. Nothing comes from your comfort zone. It's where dreams go to die.

My crew and I would absolutely fucking smash these workouts. We just had that mentality of "Fuck it. I'm going to be up at four in the morning. You got my fucking word. I got this." As a child growing up, my father told me my word was everything. The most simple form of motivation that I tell people is, "Remember your fucking word and who you said it to."

If you say one time that you'll fucking do something, that should hold true with you for your entire fucking life. If you've ever looked down on the next man for something he's not doing—as if he's lesser than you—then you automatically need to hold yourself true to what you are expecting him to be, as you're fucking persecuting him. That's just integrity. In order to not be a hypocrite, you need to hold yourself to that character across the board.

Soft motherfuckers are born right when the shit gets hard, when adversity gets thick. When the shit hits the fan, you see a true soft-ass fake motherfucker emerge. However, when you're faced with everything life can throw your way and you still stand the fuck up, this is what matters.

If you were locked up for a stretch and you returned to the world shot-out, then your time ran a fucking train over you. I don't give a shit anyway because there were two ways to do it: (1) the real motherfucking way, and (2) the bitch-ass way, coming out with them titties and a dope habit. You should have been on a fucking PC yard. That's my fucking opinion. I know plenty who didn't leave shot-out. They have my respect. The rules that garner respect for us in this life are non-negotiable. When you finally learn to *be* the man you needed your whole life, everything starts to take shape.

Remember your fucking word and who you said it to.

On most yards it's the youngsters cracking shit off. I always gravitated toward them because I had love for them. I saw more in them. I knew I could help change them. My boy Books was twenty-four when we met. Skinny, blond-haired youngster with no tattoos, from Perris, California. He was down for eight years due to an armed robbery at eighteen or nineteen. One New Year's Eve we did four fucking straight hours of burpees just to end the year with a fucking bang. Honestly, I set out to break him with a heart check while everyone watched in the dayroom. I was waiting till he tapped. But guess the fuck what? He wouldn't tap. After those four hours, with his bloodshot eyes, I told him, "Man, you're good. You got my respect for life. I love you, dog." He was strong and he was smart. His conduct matched his character.

Maybe you grew up with money troubles like me. Maybe your family was just living check to check. One day you think to yourself, *Hey, I'm going to help everyone by slangin'* (selling drugs). Trust and believe, it won't fucking work for you. Never expect a positive outcome from negative actions. You're better off playing the long view. You're better off playing the smart route, rather than finding out later how painful the penitentiary is. Long view will always pay off in the end. It does not pay off in the end to be the fake-hard motherfucker playing with his freedom.

I want you to keep this in your fucking heart: bad men are full of repentance. They look tough, and you might even think they are. They might fucking fool you, but those motherfuckers cry just like everybody else. Behind bars, they go break it down. They cry about everything they miss and they come back to the streets with that fake-ass façade, telling you, "I never cried in prison. I was the big dog, and it didn't faze me. I'm fucking badass." And yet they are the bitch with straight titties talking bad on another man because they can't just make the positive changes needed to thrive.

Long view will always pay off in the end. It does not pay off in the end to be the fake-hard motherfucker playing with his freedom.

Check your conduct. As a firm believer in these universal truths—karmic debt and cosmic justice—I believe we need to put off the correct vibe. The law of attraction is real, and we need to trust one another. Through that trust we draw in people who, in turn, trust us. When your character is at the height of who you are, everybody is subconsciously picking up on who you are and the energy you put off. In all reality, where we find validation within our hearts is what others want from us.

As I shared at the beginning of this chapter, not trusting people right off the bat is so foolish. Doing so means you're negatively dictating all the circumstances and events that could take place if this became a solid relationship. For me, everyone starts at 100 percent. It's up to them if they partake in actions that lower that percentage of trust. Please always understand that their trust percentage can always be regained through accountability. Most likely, they will only work toward earning that if they answer the call of their conscience.

In all reality, where we find validation within our hearts is what others want from us.

NO DAYS OFF!

I'm known for taking no days off. That's because I love it. I need it. It starts my day off right. Where did I learn this? You should know the answer by now: the penitentiary. There are no fucking days off in the penitentiary. You can't even opt out of a shower without getting your ass beat. If you smell bad enough and you want to rack ride and sit there stinking and you're a white boy, you're getting your shit fucking handed to you. They'll tell you, "I'm giving you some soap and a towel right now. Get your motherfucking ass in there." If you don't comply, obviously you know what time it is.

No days off. Every time that door opens—whether it's for chow, yard, or any facility movement—you're stepping out. You cannot opt out of yard. You cannot opt out of your workout. By now, this just instilled it in me. I learned the hard way. Of course, you'll hit the wall where you fucking think, *I can't work out today. I feel like fucking shit.* But when you're forced to commit, you see the benefit in it.

Progression is life.

The pump is the cure. The second you get your blood flowing, the second you climb that hurdle you couldn't and didn't want to climb, that's when it means something. The work instills the fucking worth. There is no way around that motherfucker. For any fucking thing, it means more if you feel you can't do it, but you still choose to push through. It means fucking nothing if it's easy for you.

I consistently stress "Progression is life." If you break it down to the simplest of times in my life, progressing was as simple as, "I can't fucking do it today. I feel physically beat to death. I feel like shit. But. I. Need. To." Following through was a massive amount of progression mentally. I was overcoming that self-imposed ceiling. I was climbing barriers I invented in my mind through shitty self-talk.

No days off. Think back on your own fucking challenges. Your internal dialogue yells that you can't, yet you still fucking do. How proud are you of yourself when you see something as impossible in your heart, but you still fucking do it? That's everything in this life.

History is filled with people who were so fucking close to accomplishing their goals when they tapped the fuck out. They hit that bell on the table. Ding! "I'm a bitch. I'm a fuckin' bitch. Let me the fuck out. Bitch time." Ding. Everybody was so close to making it. So many motherfuckers get so close to being a stronger dude and really killing it in their program and being respected by their people, but they bitch up. Now they'll go follow someone down the wrong path to a place filled with fucking anarchy and no fucking order.

No days off. This is the shit. When you force yourself up early, when you discipline yourself, and when you are in control, this is what makes you proud. This is what builds you as an individual. All too often, people tell me, "Wes, I just lost myself. I'm not even myself no more. I'm losing the fucking ability to even just have motivation." Motherfucker, every day is new. If every day you just start stacking your wins, you will build your motivation from the ground up. Stop talking to yourself that way!

Recently, someone complained to me about motivation. It was midday and I had been watching their posts all day. I told them, "Motherfucker, it's noon. You don't even got one W yet. How the fuck do you think you're supposed to feel if you don't even got one win by noon?" Holy fuck, my motherfucking ass is on twenty-five fucking wins by noon—counting my workout, my reading, all the shit I do for my work, my posts, the people I help. I'm on twenty-five-plus fucking Ws by noon. This is how we build our selves. Don't be that motherfucker who waits for outward shit, some external influence, to make their motherfucking day. You can choose to get wins all day.

When you force yourself up early, when you discipline yourself, and when you are in control, this is what makes you proud.

No days off. The second that first negative thought pops into your mind, you can choose to win or you can choose to lose. You can choose to be a bitch—ding, ding!—or you can choose to beast the fuck up. I couldn't accept the fact that I'm willingly becoming softer if I choose to sleep in and not hit my workout. And I see plenty of people at the gym with the same mindset. This is all a choice.

Fuck normal-people problems. I don't want titties. I don't want the softness. I don't want to watch my life fly by. I want my life to be a movie that a motherfucker will watch. That's the point—living a life that's worth telling. Live a life they write books about. Would you fucking watch a movie about a character who remains in the mindset, "Oh, I'm not even that stoked on my life"? What the fuck is that? I don't think you would watch it. I sure as fuck know you wouldn't read it. But if that's your life, motherfucker, that was your choice.

No days off. Everyone's got a life sentence. We all need to do life. I've had harder days out here than in the SHU. So, I understand you guys when you tell me shit. I'm not just fucking jaded to the fact that there's harder days out here than there is in the pen. It's a give and take. Everything's situational. I know it's mindset. But everyone wants the intel on what strengthens your mindset. I'll tell you right now: them motherfucking Ws, homie. Stack 'em!

I have people telling me that my tone and character make them feel weak. If you're thinking that to yourself right now, turning pages like you should, let me be 100 percent straight with you. I'm not making you feel no type of way, motherfucker. You stacked no wins today. You feel like a loser because you lost all day. It's simple. I won all day. You can't tell me I'm a loser. I've been winning by choice.

No days off. These small wins build our motherfucking confidence in every area. Spend more time holding complex thoughts and juggling variables. Spend more time not giving up when something's on the tip of your tongue, when you're right about to connect the dots, when you're right about to write that dope-ass post or that long-ass thing you've been trying to write. I'm talking about seeing shit through and not giving up at the last second in everything.

The way we view the world is a secret confession of character.

Make no assumptions. It's not always about not giving up on your wake-up time, or eating your meals, or that last rep. This is much deeper. Snoozing that alarm clock don't mean shit if you didn't give up in gathering your fucking knowledge. Taking that wheatgrass shot for *health* don't meant shit if you're still overweight and trashing yourself with negative internal dialogue due to a lack of results from not understanding macros. That rep don't mean shit if you're further understanding that mind-muscle connection.

There are no days off when you're walking the path of creating the individual you admire. I say this because you need to ensure that creation is implemented in all the ways that make you proud—so that your confidence is earned. When it's earned, you will have respect and love for self. In turn, all the attributes you create within, you can then see and magnify them in others around you, thus forever changing your perspective by simply unbiasedly acquiring what you admire.

The way we view the world is a secret confession of character. If your perspective of individuals around you is flawed, more than likely you're not fitting the bill. People who have trust issues are people who more than likely should not be trusted. Your perception of me is a reflection of you. Because I know that I'm a trustworthy person, I trust others.

So, how many Ws you got today? You're reading this book, that's at least one. Take a step toward earning that self-love. That's another. Take another step toward admitting your character. Take a fucking moment with yourself and admit your secret confession of character. Admit where you're not fitting the bill. That's a W.

No days off.

AFTERWORD

(Stay Fucking Hungry)

If you look in the mirror and you don't identify with that person you see in the mirror, you can never be in complete alignment.

Audra Morgan was my best friend when I got busted. Today, she's actually the wife of one of my childhood friends. She was an actress and a model when she started having issues, but she didn't know where they were coming from. People thought it was substance abuse, and everybody who was on her case about it didn't know if she was telling the truth about how she felt and about everything happening. Then she was diagnosed with multiple sclerosis.

Her story doesn't end with the doctors discovering her condition. In the process of administering a spinal tap, they left Audra paralyzed from the waist down. She'll never walk again due to a severe fuck-up in the midst of a routine procedure. Her story doesn't fucking end there either.

Three years into my sentence, she wrote a letter to me, letting me know what had happened to her. There I was in the confinement of prison while she was confined to a wheelchair. We were both going through the absolute biggest struggles of our lives.

She wrote me just in agony, trying to figure out how she would get through this. We would continually support each other daily through phone calls and through the mail when I was on lockdown and couldn't get to a phone. She was actually the only person who came to visit me the entire time. She would travel in a van that she drove by herself with only hand controls. She went out of her way, long distance, just to visit me.

After going so far, the cops would then search her in her wheelchair as if she were transporting drugs and contraband into the prison. She looked very healthy, she had tattoos, she's a beautiful woman, and they just could not get past the idea that she must be doing something shady. All this was not what it seemed. As it was with so many people in her life, the assumption was that she was a drug abuser, that she must have been using this multiple sclerosis pain to get pills and medication. In all reality, she just wanted her life back.

Our resolve to support and encourage one another continues to this day, be it over the phone, through texts, or in person. We actually went to lunch the other day—her, my wife, and me. We talked about our progress. Each of us have encountered drug abuse and problems, and we've all overcome them. It's just such a massive thing for us all to be there together.

I know everybody has pain. And I fucking
refuse to believe that they don't want to work
on it and cure everything that ails them.

For many years, I told Audra that I felt like Gru from *Despicable Me*. In prison, you will see the same movies on TV over and over and over. While I never watched any movies, I sure as fuck watched *Despicable Me* because the main character, Gru, adopts these three girls. For whatever reason, I just identified with wanting to have children so bad. It brought tears to my eyes every time I watched this movie. Later, I ended up being the stepfather to my wife's son, Wolf. Audra actually calls me Gru now; it all just came full circle.

Nevertheless, it was so massive how everything took place. We just always sought to better ourselves and be each other's accountability partner. When the other one was feeling down, we would pick them up. That's exactly what I brought out to society today. I know what pain is. I know everybody has pain. And I fucking refuse to believe that they don't want to work on it and cure everything that ails them.

I have the solution and it's not easy, but it's definitely possible. I've seen some people do it in a matter of weeks, and some people never pull it off at all. Through my program, my crew and I were able to accomplish growth in mind, body, and soul by truly stepping right in front of this pain and confronting it, by not letting the inaction that so many fall victim to be the paralyzation and the prison that we live in.

Audra was that mental accountability partner for me over the phone during my entire incarceration. I just needed to bring that to the guys around me in prison. I brought that positivity, discipline, and ability to change to them and packaged it with the physical endeavors we would pursue every day. So, what I ended up showing them was that this is how people found themselves and their purpose. Since the dawn of time, the meaning of life had been discovered through massive reflection, enduring extreme applications of physical activity, and the actual limitation of foods.

If you want to get up in the morning to be your best every day, I've put together the program for you that works on building your discipline.

Back in the day, people would seek solitude. They would go on extreme treks and they would fast. Honestly, my program was the 2015 approach to the same goals. Today, after 2020 and the COVID-19 lockdowns, everyone knows solitude.

Most people just focused on the part where they couldn't go outside. But that meant we kept ourselves in the now; we stayed present more. You focus on what you can do now. You weren't drifting past the fences, chains, and barbed wire into anything outside your reach.

In my program, I teach you the process that taps into your purpose. It taps into mind, body, and soul growth. We're all too focused on external gratification and getting it right now—the right career, the right partner, and fucking so on—instead of becoming it. If you want to attract the right career, you need to become the right candidate. We must seek to become valuable, and success will chase us instead of us chasing success. If you want to attract the right partner, you need to become the right partner. If you want to get up in the morning to be your best every day, I've put together the program for you that works on building your discipline.

As we approach the end of *Non-Negotiable*, it's crystal fucking clear that discipline is the key to success in everything. Your level of success will never exceed your level of personal development. This all comes from discipline. Our personal development comes from our level of discipline to seek the areas where we're weak and overcome them in order to develop into the best person we can possibly be in order to excel in everything that we encounter.

Of course, people are continually dropping the ball because they think you can just read about this shit. My book won't magically teach you everything and provide those break-throughs. The intention behind my writing is to provide the mindset tactics for you to then put into motherfucking action. The action is what breaks you through to the outcome.

When we combine this wisdom of the ancients, we actually learn both through active experience and self-reflection—magnifying our self-talk during these workouts and while we're hungry. It just gets louder and louder and we're able to really decipher what's going on inside of ourselves. This leads to control.

Control is what everyone's actually pursuing. We can negate all vices and all issues or problems if we are truly in control and stick to the plan. And that's exactly what I fucking teach. I enable the people who don't even know what a macro is to become masters of their nutrition and diet in a very short time. This is the key to self-mastery. When they're able to transfer mastery in the diet and nutrition department onto other areas of their lives, this causes the alignment needed to fulfill both their complete vision of where they're going and who they feel they are—mind, body, and soul.

It's not okay to stay stuck in the future and suffer the pain of anxiety over and over, day in and day out.

As I wrote this book, the COVID-19 pandemic was still going strong. This resulted in lockdowns for most of us. I imagine many of you have never experienced a life where you couldn't go to work, where you were stuck in your house, where businesses weren't open. Well, fuck. I've been in lockdowns before. I know how massive it is to stay strong mentally, physically, and spiritually. The crazy part is that every lockdown in the penitentiary was followed by race riots. It's just what happens. They segregate and separate. To come out to the real world and see this taking place in 2020 was just mind-boggling to me.

If you're feeling imprisoned, you're not alone. I've been there. But it's up to you to break through all these negative mental blocks with your discipline and commitment to a daily process, personal development, and a personal growth process.

And if you're feeling uncertain of the world in the future, you're not alone, because we're all uncertain. This had never happened before. We'd never been on a worldwide lockdown—so your uncertainty is justified. But it's not okay to stay stuck in the future and suffer the pain of anxiety over and over, day in and day out.

If your heart is strong, you have the basis of alignment.

What must be done is focusing on the now, creating the best possible individual you can, so that you can bring that to everybody around you. Doing so means we can lift our collective rate of vibration and bring up everybody around us to find positive solutions and get the outcomes we need to get through this.

Each of us gets in our own way on a regular basis. From one simple, massive flaw, we're choosing a negative thought over a positive one. So, what makes us strong enough to put the positive spin on any negative event? Ding! Discipline. It's our mind. It's our choices. We must make the choice and spin it in our favor to get that positive outcome because life is always happening for you. If you can build a strong foundation within your mind, body, and soul, that foundation will always be there to make this choice. If your heart is strong, you have the basis of alignment.

I wish you all well. I want you to seek purpose over pleasure in your day with every daily choice you make. Seek purpose over pleasure and let that become your ultimate pleasure. When constructing your vision, you must always unbiasedly acquire what you admire so that you don't end up creating a vision that you weren't even after—or falling victim to societal standards that don't resonate in your heart. Such outcomes can be further avoided in the construction of supportive habits and focusing on the power of gratitude to tap into infinite intelligence.

And, by all means, in the end the goal is to find what we're best at. When you have finally found that for yourself, I want you to give that to the world by personifying the teaching. That's mandatory.

We master every day when we string together perfect days.

It's non-negotiable to conduct yourself in this manner every day. You are constructing that person through your daily steps. The man who takes pride in his daily steps, who visualizes who he must become, and then sees it through by committing to discipline is a man who's creating something much more powerful than his current belief.

In closing, the program is not meant for an aesthetic standpoint. The point isn't about making you look so great. Yes, that's a byproduct. There are no days off from character construction, no days off from solidifying your core beliefs in order to make it through your day without any speed bumps totally derailing you from your goals. It's no days off because this is how we create the individual we truly admire, and in the end, we share that person with the world.

Can you go give your workout 100 percent?
Motherfucker, it's harder not to.

We master every day when we string together perfect days. Everything is possible in this life. The only shit that should be up for negotiation is not being accountable when we're supposed to be perfect. And don't get me started on the shitty-ass mindset, "Oh but Wes, no one is perfect."

Fuck that. Fuck that shit. I guarantee you could be perfect on 95 percent of the shit in your day that's holding you back. Think about it. Can you perfect your wake-up time? Yeah, motherfucker, you can. Can you perfect your meals? Fuck yeah, you can. Can you go give your workout 100 percent? Motherfucker, it's harder not to.

Beyond the closing of this final page, we're going to wake up every day. We're going to create the process that's optimal to get us to the highest character, the highest quality physique, and the highest ability to work toward our goals. We will become a quality fucking product for those we love. This ain't for just you. Make your fucking kids proud. Make your parents proud. Make your people proud.

Stay fucking hungry. Keep *fighting*. And live a life worth living.

Put this shit down and earn your Ws.

Let's fucking get this.

ABOUT THE AUTHOR

From serving nearly a decade in the California State Penitentiary system to building a highly successful online coaching business that has impacted the lives of tens of thousands of people all around the world, Wes Watson is far from your typical success story. With over 60 million views and nearly half a million subscribers on his YouTube channel, his strong message and worldview has captivated a global audience.

Incarceration led him on a journey of deep introspection. In turn, his focus shifted toward living a life for a greater purpose. He's now dedicated to serving others and sharing his no-bullshit, tough-love advice to help them do the same. Featured in *NY Post* and Business Insider, Wes has also appeared in a number of notable podcasts for his deep insight on life lessons he's learned from his hard past. He's made it his mission to help others expand their consciousness and to motivate millions to live a life of purpose.

CPSIA information can be obtained
at www.ICGtesting.com
Printed in the USA
LVHW080055231022
731317LV00011B/655